Cybersecurity for Businesses

What managers need to know

December 2024

Dr Alex Bugeja, PhD

Introduction

Introduction

In today's interconnected world, cybersecurity is no longer just an IT issue; it's a fundamental business concern. Every organization, regardless of size or industry, is a potential target for cyberattacks. The consequences of a security breach can be devastating, ranging from financial losses and reputational damage to legal liabilities and operational disruptions. As a manager, you play a critical role in safeguarding your organization's digital assets and ensuring its resilience in the face of evolving cyber threats.

This book, "Cybersecurity for Businesses: What Managers Need to Know," is designed to provide you with a comprehensive understanding of the cybersecurity landscape and equip you with the knowledge and tools to effectively manage cyber risks within your organization. We will delve into the various aspects of cybersecurity, from identifying common threats and vulnerabilities to implementing robust security measures and fostering a culture of security awareness among your employees.

The digital age has brought unprecedented opportunities for businesses, but it has also introduced a new set of challenges. The increasing reliance on technology, coupled with the growing sophistication of cybercriminals, has created a complex and dynamic threat environment. Cyberattacks are no longer limited to large corporations or government agencies; small and medium-sized businesses are increasingly targeted, often with devastating consequences.

As a manager, you may not be a cybersecurity expert, but you need to have a solid understanding of the key concepts and principles to make informed decisions and guide your organization's cybersecurity strategy. This book aims to bridge the gap between the technical complexities of cybersecurity and the practical needs of business leaders. We will avoid jargon and technical deep dives, focusing instead on providing clear, concise explanations and actionable insights that you can apply to your organization.

Throughout this book, we will explore the various dimensions of cybersecurity, starting with an overview of the current threat landscape. We will examine the motivations and tactics of cybercriminals, the types of attacks they employ, and the potential impact on businesses. Understanding the "enemy" is the first step in developing an effective defense strategy.

Next, we will discuss how to identify and assess your organization's digital assets. These are the crown jewels that cybercriminals seek to steal, disrupt, or destroy. Understanding what you need to protect is crucial in prioritizing your security efforts and allocating resources effectively.

We will then delve into the common cyber threats and attack vectors that businesses face. From phishing and malware to ransomware and denial-of-service attacks, we will explore the various ways in which cybercriminals can infiltrate your systems and compromise your data.

Once you have a clear understanding of the threats and your vulnerabilities, we will guide you through the process of assessing your organization's cybersecurity risk. This involves evaluating the likelihood and potential impact of different types of attacks, taking into account your specific industry, business model, and technology infrastructure.

With a comprehensive risk assessment in hand, we will move on to building a robust cybersecurity strategy. This involves defining your security objectives, identifying the appropriate controls and countermeasures, and establishing a framework for ongoing monitoring and improvement.

Implementing a security framework, such as those defined by NIST, will provide a structured approach to managing cybersecurity risk. While we won't cover frameworks in a "how-to" manner, we will provide an overview of the key components and principles, enabling you to make informed decisions about their implementation within your organization.

Data protection and privacy regulations, such as the General Data Protection Regulation (GDPR) and the California Consumer Privacy Act (CCPA), are increasingly important considerations for businesses. We will explore the key requirements of these regulations and their implications for your cybersecurity practices.

Network security is a fundamental aspect of any cybersecurity program. We will discuss the basic principles of network security, including firewalls, intrusion detection systems, and virtual private networks (VPNs), and how they can be used to protect your organization's network perimeter.

Endpoint protection focuses on securing the devices that connect to your network, such as laptops, desktops, and mobile devices. We will explore the various threats to endpoints and the measures you can take to mitigate them, including antivirus software, endpoint detection and response (EDR) solutions, and mobile device management (MDM) platforms.

Cloud computing has revolutionized the way businesses operate, but it also introduces new security challenges. We will discuss the unique security considerations of cloud environments, including shared responsibility models, data encryption, and access controls.

Identity and access management (IAM) is a critical component of any cybersecurity program. We will explore the principles of IAM, including authentication, authorization, and privileged access management, and how they can be used to control access to your organization's sensitive data and systems.

Employees are often the weakest link in the security chain. Security awareness training is essential to educate your workforce about the various cyber threats they may encounter and how to recognize and respond to them. We will discuss the key elements of an effective security awareness program and provide practical tips for engaging your employees.

No matter how well-prepared you are, security incidents can still occur. Incident response planning is crucial to minimize the impact of a breach and ensure a swift and effective recovery. We will guide you through the process of developing an incident response plan, including roles and responsibilities, communication protocols, and forensic analysis procedures.

Disaster recovery and business continuity are closely related to incident response. We will discuss the importance of having a plan in place to recover from major disruptions, such as natural disasters or cyberattacks, and how to ensure the continuity of your critical business operations.

Vulnerability management and penetration testing are proactive measures that can help you identify and address security weaknesses before they are exploited by cybercriminals. We will explore the different types of vulnerabilities and the methods for assessing and mitigating them.

Secure software development lifecycle (SSDLC) is a process for building security into software applications from the ground up. We will discuss the key principles of SSDLC and how they can be integrated into your software development processes.

Third-party risk management is increasingly important as businesses rely more heavily on external vendors and service providers. We will explore the potential security risks associated with third parties and the measures you can take to assess and manage them.

Encryption is a powerful tool for protecting sensitive data, both in transit and at rest. We will discuss the different types of encryption and their applications in securing your organization's data.

Mobile security is a growing concern as more and more employees use their personal devices for work purposes. We will explore the unique security challenges of mobile devices and the best practices for securing them.

The Internet of Things (IoT) is rapidly expanding, with billions of connected devices being deployed in homes, businesses, and industrial settings. We will discuss the security implications of IoT and the measures you can take to protect your organization from IoT-related threats.

Social engineering is a technique used by cybercriminals to manipulate individuals into divulging sensitive information or performing actions that compromise security. We will explore the various social engineering tactics and how to educate your employees to recognize and resist them.

Cybersecurity insurance is becoming increasingly popular as a way to mitigate the financial risks associated with cyberattacks. We will discuss the different types of cybersecurity insurance policies and the factors to consider when choosing coverage.

Monitoring and auditing your security posture is essential to ensure that your controls are effective and that your systems are secure. We will explore the various monitoring and auditing techniques and how they can be used to improve your overall security posture.

The cybersecurity landscape is constantly evolving, with new threats and vulnerabilities emerging all the time. We will discuss the importance of staying ahead of emerging threats and the resources available to help you do so.

Finally, we will emphasize the importance of building a cybersecurity culture within your organization. This involves creating a shared sense of responsibility for security, fostering open communication about security issues, and providing ongoing training and awareness programs.

By the end of this book, you will have a comprehensive understanding of the cybersecurity landscape, the key concepts and principles, and the practical steps you can take to protect your organization from cyber threats. You will be equipped to make informed decisions about cybersecurity strategy, allocate resources effectively, and foster a culture of security awareness among your employees. Remember, cybersecurity is not just an IT issue; it's a business imperative. By taking a proactive and informed approach to cybersecurity, you can protect your organization's digital assets, maintain the trust of your customers and partners, and ensure your continued success in the digital age.

CHAPTER ONE: Understanding the Cybersecurity Landscape

In the modern business environment, digital interconnectivity is not just an advantage, it's a necessity. Companies rely on networks, software, and the internet for everything from communication and data storage to sales and customer service. This digital transformation has brought immense benefits, including increased efficiency, wider market reach, and enhanced customer engagement. However, this reliance on technology has also opened the door to a host of new threats collectively known as cyber threats. These threats are no longer a niche problem confined to the IT department. They are a pervasive and evolving risk that every manager needs to understand and address.

The cybersecurity landscape is a complex and dynamic environment shaped by a variety of factors, including technological advancements, geopolitical tensions, and the ever-changing tactics of cybercriminals. It's a world where malicious actors, often operating with sophisticated tools and techniques, seek to exploit vulnerabilities in systems and networks for financial gain, espionage, or simply to cause disruption. The targets are diverse, ranging from multinational corporations and government agencies to small businesses and even individuals. No one is immune to the threat, and the consequences of a successful attack can be severe.

One of the key challenges in understanding the cybersecurity landscape is the sheer pace of change. New technologies are constantly emerging, creating new opportunities for both businesses and cybercriminals. The rise of cloud computing, mobile devices, and the Internet of Things (IoT) has expanded the attack surface, providing more entry points for malicious actors to exploit. At the same time, cybercriminals are constantly developing new methods of attack, making it difficult for organizations to keep up. What was considered a secure system yesterday may be vulnerable today.

Another factor contributing to the complexity of the cybersecurity landscape is the diverse nature of the threats. Cyberattacks can take many forms, from simple phishing emails designed to trick employees into revealing sensitive information to sophisticated ransomware attacks that encrypt critical data and demand payment for its release. Some attacks are targeted, focusing on a specific organization or individual, while others are opportunistic, seeking to exploit any vulnerable system they can find. The motivations of cybercriminals also vary, ranging from financial gain to political activism to espionage.

The actors behind these threats are equally diverse. They include organized crime syndicates, state-sponsored hackers, hacktivists, and even disgruntled insiders. Some operate independently, while others are part of larger networks. They may be highly skilled professionals with access to advanced resources, or they may be amateurs using readily available tools and techniques. This diversity of actors and motivations makes it difficult to predict where the next threat will come from or what form it will take.

The impact of cyberattacks on businesses can be far-reaching. Financial losses can result from theft of funds, extortion payments, or the cost of recovering from an attack. Reputational damage can occur if customer data is compromised or if the attack becomes public knowledge. Legal liabilities may arise if the organization fails to comply with data protection regulations or if it is found to have been negligent in its security practices. Operational disruptions can occur if critical systems are taken offline or if data is lost or corrupted. In some cases, a severe cyberattack can even threaten the very survival of a business.

In addition to the direct impact on businesses, cyberattacks can also have broader societal consequences. Attacks on critical infrastructure, such as power grids or transportation systems, can disrupt essential services and even endanger public safety. Attacks on government agencies can compromise sensitive information and undermine national security. The increasing interconnectedness of our world means that a cyberattack in one part of the globe can have ripple effects across the entire system.

To effectively manage cybersecurity risk, it's essential to understand the motivations and tactics of cybercriminals. Why do they do what they do? What are they looking for? How do they operate? By understanding the "enemy," you can better anticipate their actions and develop more effective defenses.

One of the primary motivations of cybercriminals is financial gain. They may seek to steal money directly from bank accounts, or they may steal sensitive data, such as credit card numbers or personal information, that they can sell on the dark web. They may also use ransomware to encrypt data and demand payment for its release. The potential profits from cybercrime are enormous, and the risks are often perceived as being relatively low.

Another motivation is espionage. State-sponsored hackers may target government agencies or businesses to steal sensitive information, such as trade secrets or military plans. This type of cyber espionage can give a country a strategic advantage in both the economic and military spheres.

Hacktivism is another driver of cyberattacks. Hacktivists are individuals or groups who use hacking to promote a political or social agenda. They may target organizations or individuals they perceive as being unethical or corrupt, or they may seek to disrupt systems or services as a form of protest.

Some cybercriminals are simply motivated by the challenge of breaking into systems or causing disruption. They may see it as a game or a test of their skills. These "script kiddies," as they are sometimes called, may not have a specific target in mind but may simply be looking for any vulnerable system they can exploit.

Regardless of their motivations, cybercriminals use a variety of tactics to achieve their goals. One of the most common is social engineering, which involves manipulating individuals into divulging sensitive information or performing actions that compromise security. This can be done through phishing emails, phone calls, or even in-person interactions.

Another common tactic is malware, which is short for malicious software. Malware can take many forms, including viruses, worms, trojans, and ransomware. It can be delivered through email attachments, infected websites, or compromised software downloads. Once installed on a system, malware can steal data, disrupt operations, or even take control of the system.

Cybercriminals also exploit vulnerabilities in software and hardware. These vulnerabilities can be flaws in the design of a system or errors in the code. They can allow attackers to gain unauthorized access to a system, execute malicious code, or steal data.

Denial-of-service (DoS) attacks are another tactic used by cybercriminals. These attacks aim to overwhelm a system or network with traffic, making it unavailable to legitimate users. This can disrupt business operations and cause financial losses.

Advanced persistent threats (APTs) are a more sophisticated form of attack. They involve a long-term, targeted campaign to infiltrate a specific organization's network and steal sensitive data. APTs are often carried out by state-sponsored actors and can be very difficult to detect and defend against.

The cybersecurity landscape is constantly evolving, with new threats and vulnerabilities emerging all the time. To stay ahead of the curve, it's essential to be aware of the latest trends and developments.

One trend is the increasing use of artificial intelligence (AI) by both cybercriminals and security professionals. AI can be used to automate attacks, making them faster and more efficient. It can also be used to develop more sophisticated malware that can evade detection. On the other hand, AI can also be used to enhance security defenses, by detecting anomalies in network traffic or identifying patterns that indicate an attack is underway.

Another trend is the growing use of cloud computing. While cloud services offer many benefits, they also introduce new security challenges. Organizations need to ensure that their data is properly secured in the cloud and that access is appropriately controlled.

The Internet of Things (IoT) is another area of concern. The increasing number of connected devices, from smart thermostats to industrial control systems, creates a vast attack surface. Many of these devices have weak security, making them vulnerable to attack.

Mobile security is also becoming increasingly important as more and more employees use their personal devices for work purposes. Organizations need to develop policies and procedures to ensure that these devices are properly secured and that sensitive data is protected.

The rise of cryptocurrencies has also had an impact on the cybersecurity landscape. Cryptocurrencies are often used by cybercriminals for ransomware payments or to launder money obtained through illegal activities. The decentralized nature of cryptocurrencies makes them difficult to trace, which can make it harder to catch and prosecute cybercriminals.

Finally, the geopolitical landscape is also playing a role in shaping the cybersecurity threat environment. Tensions between countries can lead to an increase in state-sponsored cyberattacks. These attacks can target government agencies, critical infrastructure, or even private businesses.

Understanding the cybersecurity landscape is not just about knowing the threats; it's also about understanding the defenses. There are many tools and techniques available to help organizations protect themselves from cyberattacks. These include firewalls, intrusion detection systems, antivirus software, and encryption.

However, technology alone is not enough. A comprehensive cybersecurity strategy must also include policies, procedures, and training. Organizations need to develop clear guidelines for how employees should handle sensitive data, how they should use technology, and how they should respond to security incidents.

Employee training is particularly important, as employees are often the weakest link in the security chain. They need to be educated about the various cyber threats they may encounter and how to recognize and respond to them.

Another important aspect of cybersecurity is incident response planning. No matter how well-prepared you are, security incidents can still occur. Having a plan in place to deal with these incidents can minimize the impact and ensure a swift and effective recovery.

The cybersecurity landscape is complex and constantly changing. As a manager, you don't need to be a technical expert, but you do need to have a basic understanding of the threats and the defenses. By staying informed about the latest trends and developments, you can help your organization develop a robust cybersecurity strategy and protect its valuable assets.

The world of cybersecurity is full of jargon and technical terms that can be confusing to the uninitiated. As we delve deeper into the subject in the following chapters, we will encounter many of these terms. But for now, let's just clarify a few key concepts that will be important throughout this book.

First, let's define what we mean by "cybersecurity." Cybersecurity is the practice of protecting computer systems, networks, and data from unauthorized access, use, disclosure, disruption, modification, or destruction. It encompasses a wide range of technologies, processes, and practices designed to safeguard digital assets from cyber threats.

A "cyber threat" is any potential danger to a computer system, network, or data. This can include malicious software (malware), phishing attacks, denial-of-service attacks, and many other types of attacks.

A "vulnerability" is a weakness in a system or network that can be exploited by a cyber threat. This can be a flaw in the design of a system, an error in the code, or even a lack of proper security procedures.

An "attack vector" is the path or means by which a cybercriminal gains access to a system or network. This can be an email attachment, a compromised website, or a vulnerable software application.

"Risk" in the context of cybersecurity refers to the likelihood that a cyber threat will exploit a vulnerability and cause harm to an organization. It is often expressed as a combination of the probability of an attack occurring and the potential impact of that attack.

"Mitigation" refers to the measures taken to reduce or eliminate cybersecurity risks. This can include implementing security controls, patching vulnerabilities, and training employees.

These are just a few of the key terms we will be using throughout this book. As we explore each topic in more detail, we will introduce other terms and concepts as needed. But for now, having a basic understanding of these terms will help you navigate the complex world of cybersecurity.

The cybersecurity landscape is not static; it's a dynamic and ever-evolving environment. What was considered a secure system yesterday may be vulnerable today. New technologies are constantly emerging, creating new opportunities for both businesses and cybercriminals. The tactics of cybercriminals are also constantly changing, as they seek new ways to exploit vulnerabilities and evade detection.

To stay ahead of the curve, it's essential to be aware of the latest trends and developments in the cybersecurity landscape. This includes staying informed about new threats, new vulnerabilities, and new security technologies. It also means understanding the changing motivations and tactics of cybercriminals.

There are many resources available to help you stay informed about cybersecurity. These include industry publications, security blogs, and government reports. Many security vendors also provide valuable information about the latest threats and vulnerabilities.

Attending industry conferences and events can also be a good way to stay up-to-date on the latest trends and developments. These events often feature presentations by leading experts in the field and provide opportunities to network with other professionals.

Another important aspect of staying ahead of the curve is to regularly assess your organization's cybersecurity posture. This involves evaluating your current security controls, identifying any weaknesses or gaps, and making necessary improvements.

The cybersecurity landscape is a complex and challenging environment. But by understanding the threats, the defenses, and the latest trends, you can help your organization develop a robust cybersecurity strategy and protect its valuable assets. As we move forward through the rest of this book, we will delve deeper into each of these areas, providing you with the knowledge and tools you need to effectively manage cybersecurity risk within your organization. The journey to a more secure digital future begins with understanding the landscape we are navigating. It's a landscape filled with challenges, but also with opportunities. By embracing a proactive and informed approach to cybersecurity, businesses can not only protect themselves from threats but also build trust with their customers, partners, and stakeholders. This trust is essential for success in the digital age, where reputation and reliability are paramount.

CHAPTER TWO: Identifying Your Business's Digital Assets

In the realm of cybersecurity, understanding what you need to protect is just as crucial as knowing how to protect it. Your business's digital assets are the lifeblood of your operations, the currency of the digital age. They are the valuable data, systems, and applications that enable your business to function, compete, and thrive. Identifying these assets is the first step towards building a robust cybersecurity strategy. It's a fundamental process that lays the groundwork for all subsequent security measures. Without a clear understanding of what your digital assets are, you're essentially operating in the dark, unable to prioritize your security efforts or allocate resources effectively.

So, what exactly are digital assets? In simple terms, they are any information or systems that hold value to your organization and are stored or processed in a digital format. This can range from sensitive customer data and financial records to intellectual property and critical business applications. It can also include the hardware and infrastructure that support these digital assets, such as servers, networks, and endpoint devices.

To identify your digital assets, you need to take a comprehensive inventory of your organization's information and systems. This is not just an IT exercise; it requires collaboration across different departments to ensure that no critical assets are overlooked. You need to involve business unit leaders, legal counsel, human resources, and other key stakeholders to get a complete picture of your organization's digital landscape.

Let's start with the most obvious category of digital assets: data. Data is the raw material of the digital economy. It's the information that your business collects, processes, and stores. This can include customer data, such as names, addresses, contact information, and purchase history. It can also include financial data, such as bank account details, credit card numbers, and transaction records.

Employee data is another important category. This includes personal information, such as social security numbers, payroll data, and performance reviews. You may also have sensitive intellectual property, such as trade secrets, patents, and proprietary software code.

In addition to data, your digital assets also include the systems and applications that process and store this data. These can be customer relationship management (CRM) systems, enterprise resource planning (ERP) systems, accounting software, and email servers. They can also include custom-built applications that are specific to your business.

The hardware and infrastructure that support these systems are also considered digital assets. This includes servers, network devices, storage systems, and endpoint devices, such as laptops, desktops, and mobile phones. These physical components are essential for the functioning of your digital operations and need to be protected accordingly.

Once you have a comprehensive inventory of your digital assets, the next step is to classify them based on their value and sensitivity. Not all assets are created equal. Some are more critical to your business operations than others. Some contain more sensitive information than others. Classifying your assets helps you prioritize your security efforts and allocate resources effectively.

A common approach to classifying digital assets is to use a three-tiered system: high, medium, and low. High-value assets are those that are critical to your business operations or contain highly sensitive information. These could be your customer database, your financial systems, or your intellectual property. A compromise of these assets could have a severe impact on your business, potentially leading to financial losses, reputational damage, or legal liabilities.

Medium-value assets are those that are important to your business operations but are not as critical as high-value assets. They may contain moderately sensitive information. A compromise of these assets could cause some disruption to your business but would not be as severe as a compromise of high-value assets.

Low-value assets are those that are not critical to your business operations and do not contain sensitive information. A compromise of these assets would have a minimal impact on your business.

It's important to note that the classification of assets is not a one-size-fits-all process. What is considered a high-value asset for one organization may be a low-value asset for another. The classification should be based on your specific business context, taking into account your industry, your business model, and your risk tolerance.

Once you have classified your assets, you can start to map them to your business processes. This helps you understand how each asset is used and how a compromise of that asset could impact your business. For example, you might find that your customer database is used by your sales team to generate leads, by your marketing team to run campaigns, and by your customer service team to resolve issues. A compromise of this database could disrupt all of these processes, leading to lost sales, ineffective marketing, and poor customer service.

Mapping your assets to your business processes also helps you identify single points of failure. These are assets that, if compromised, could bring down multiple processes or even your entire business. For example, if your email server is a single point of failure for all internal and external communications, a compromise of that server could cripple your ability to communicate with employees, customers, and partners.

Identifying single points of failure is crucial for developing a robust business continuity plan. You need to ensure that you have backups and redundancies in place for these critical assets so that if one fails, another can take over seamlessly.

Another important aspect of identifying your digital assets is to understand where they are located. This includes both physical and logical locations. Physical locations refer to the actual physical location of the hardware that stores or processes your data. This could be your own data center, a third-party data center, or even an employee's home office.

Logical locations refer to where the data is stored within your systems. This could be a specific database, a file server, or a cloud storage service. Understanding the location of your assets is important for several reasons. First, it helps you assess the physical security of your assets. If your data is stored in a secure data center with access controls and surveillance systems, it is likely to be more secure than if it is stored on a laptop in an employee's home office.

Second, understanding the location of your assets helps you comply with data privacy regulations. Some regulations, such as the General Data Protection Regulation (GDPR), require you to know where your data is stored and to ensure that it is adequately protected.

Third, knowing the location of your assets helps you respond to security incidents more effectively. If you know that a specific server contains sensitive customer data, you can quickly isolate that server in the event of a breach to prevent further data loss.

Identifying your digital assets is not a one-time exercise. It's an ongoing process that needs to be reviewed and updated regularly. As your business evolves, your digital assets will change. New systems will be implemented, new data will be collected, and new processes will be created. You need to ensure that your asset inventory and classification keep pace with these changes.

One way to ensure that your asset inventory is up-to-date is to incorporate it into your change management process. Whenever a new system is implemented, a new application is deployed, or a new process is created, you should assess the impact on your digital assets and update your inventory accordingly.

Another way to keep your asset inventory current is to conduct regular audits. This involves reviewing your existing inventory, identifying any gaps or inaccuracies, and making necessary updates. Audits can be conducted internally by your IT team or externally by a third-party security firm.

Identifying your digital assets is a foundational step in building a robust cybersecurity strategy. It's a process that requires collaboration, diligence, and ongoing attention. By understanding what your digital assets are, where they are located, and how they are used, you can develop a more effective security posture and protect your business from the ever-evolving threat landscape.

It's also essential to understand the flow of data within your organization. Data doesn't just sit still; it moves between systems, applications, and people. Mapping these data flows helps you understand how data is created, processed, stored, and transmitted. This knowledge is crucial for identifying potential security risks and implementing appropriate controls.

For example, if customer data is collected through a web form, stored in a database, and then accessed by a customer service representative, you need to ensure that security controls are in place at each stage of this process. This might include encrypting the data in transit, implementing access controls on the database, and providing security awareness training to the customer service representative.

Understanding data flows also helps you comply with data privacy regulations. Some regulations require you to demonstrate that you have control over the flow of personal data within your organization. By mapping your data flows, you can show regulators that you know where your data is going and that you have implemented appropriate safeguards to protect it.

In the context of identifying your digital assets, it's also important to consider the role of third parties. Many businesses rely on external vendors and service providers for various functions, such as cloud storage, payment processing, and customer support. These third parties often have access to your digital assets, which introduces additional security risks.

When identifying your digital assets, you need to consider those that are handled by third parties. This includes understanding what data is shared with third parties, how it is shared, and how it is protected. You also need to assess the security practices of your third-party vendors to ensure that they meet your security standards.

This can be done through security questionnaires, audits, and contractual agreements. You should also have a process in place for monitoring the security performance of your third-party vendors on an ongoing basis.

Another important aspect of identifying your digital assets is to understand their value to potential attackers. Not all assets are equally attractive to cybercriminals. Some assets, such as financial data or intellectual property, are more valuable than others.

Understanding the value of your assets to attackers helps you prioritize your security efforts and allocate resources effectively. You can focus on protecting your most valuable assets first and implementing stronger controls around them.

To assess the value of your assets to attackers, you need to consider the motivations of different types of attackers. For example, financially motivated attackers might be interested in stealing credit card numbers or bank account details. State-sponsored attackers might be interested in stealing intellectual property or sensitive government information.

You also need to consider the potential impact of a compromise of each asset. If a particular asset were compromised, what would be the consequences for your business? Would it result in financial losses, reputational damage, legal liabilities, or operational disruptions?

By understanding the value of your assets to attackers and the potential impact of a compromise, you can develop a more targeted and effective security strategy.

Identifying your digital assets is a critical first step in building a robust cybersecurity program. It's a process that requires a thorough understanding of your business operations, your data, your systems, and your third-party relationships. By taking a comprehensive and systematic approach to identifying and classifying your digital assets, you can lay the foundation for a more secure and resilient organization. This process is not just about making lists; it's about gaining a deep understanding of what makes your business tick in the digital age. Once this understanding is achieved, the path towards protecting these vital components becomes clearer, allowing for strategic decision-making that aligns with both business objectives and security imperatives.

CHAPTER THREE: Common Cyber Threats and Attack Vectors

Now that we've explored the importance of understanding the cybersecurity landscape and identifying your valuable digital assets, it's time to delve into the specific threats that businesses face in the digital realm. Knowing your enemy is a fundamental principle of any security strategy, and in the world of cybersecurity, the "enemies" are the various cyber threats and attack vectors that malicious actors use to compromise systems and data. This chapter will provide an overview of the most common types of cyber threats and the methods used to deliver them, offering you a clearer picture of the dangers lurking in the digital shadows.

Think of cyber threats as the weapons in an attacker's arsenal. These can range from simple, opportunistic attacks to highly sophisticated, targeted campaigns. Understanding the nature of these threats is crucial for developing effective defenses. Just as a general needs to know the types of weapons their opponent possesses, a business manager needs to understand the types of cyber threats their organization faces.

One of the most prevalent cyber threats is malware, short for malicious software. Malware is an umbrella term that encompasses a wide range of harmful programs designed to infiltrate, damage, or disrupt computer systems and networks. There are many different types of malware, each with its own unique characteristics and methods of operation.

Viruses are perhaps the most well-known type of malware. A virus is a program that replicates itself by attaching to other files or programs. When an infected file is executed, the virus spreads to other files, potentially causing damage or disruption. Viruses can be delivered through various means, such as email attachments, infected websites, or removable media like USB drives.

Worms are similar to viruses in that they can self-replicate, but unlike viruses, they don't need to attach to other files to spread. Worms can propagate through networks, exploiting vulnerabilities in operating systems or applications to infect other connected devices. This ability to spread rapidly makes worms particularly dangerous, as they can quickly infect a large number of systems.

Trojans, named after the famous Trojan Horse of Greek mythology, are a type of malware that disguises itself as a legitimate program or file. When a user is tricked into executing the Trojan, it installs malicious code on their system, giving the attacker unauthorized access or control. Trojans can be used for various malicious purposes, such as stealing data, installing other malware, or creating a backdoor for the attacker to access the system later.

Ransomware is a particularly insidious type of malware that has gained prominence in recent years. Ransomware encrypts the victim's data, making it inaccessible, and then demands a ransom payment, usually in cryptocurrency, in exchange for the decryption key. Ransomware attacks can be devastating for businesses, as they can lead to significant financial losses, operational disruptions, and reputational damage.

Spyware is a type of malware designed to secretly monitor and collect information about a user's activities. This can include keystrokes, browsing history, passwords, and other sensitive data. Spyware can be used for various purposes, such as identity theft, corporate espionage, or even stalking.

Adware, while generally less harmful than other types of malware, can still be a nuisance. Adware is software that displays unwanted advertisements on a user's computer. These ads can be intrusive, annoying, and can even slow down the system's performance. In some cases, adware can also collect information about the user's browsing habits, raising privacy concerns.

Rootkits are a particularly stealthy type of malware that are designed to give an attacker privileged access to a system while hiding their presence from the user and even from security software. Rootkits can be very difficult to detect and remove, and they can give an attacker complete control over the infected system.

These are just a few examples of the many types of malware that exist. New variants and entirely new types of malware are constantly being developed, making it a never-ending battle to keep up with the latest threats.

Another common cyber threat is phishing. Phishing is a social engineering technique used to trick individuals into divulging sensitive information, such as usernames, passwords, or credit card details. Phishing attacks typically involve sending an email or text message that appears to be from a legitimate source, such as a bank, a government agency, or a well-known company. The message often contains a link to a fake website that mimics the look and feel of the real website. When the victim enters their credentials on the fake website, the attacker captures them.

Phishing attacks can be very effective because they exploit human psychology rather than technical vulnerabilities. They rely on the victim's trust in the apparent source of the message and their willingness to comply with the request. Phishing attacks can be generic, targeting a large number of people, or they can be highly targeted, focusing on a specific individual or organization. This latter type is known as spear phishing.

Spear phishing attacks are often more successful than generic phishing attacks because they are tailored to the specific target. The attacker may research the target beforehand to gather information that can be used to make the phishing message more convincing. For example, they may use the target's name, job title, or other personal information in the message.

Another variant of phishing is called whaling. Whaling is a type of spear phishing that targets high-profile individuals, such as CEOs, executives, or government officials. These attacks are often more sophisticated and well-funded than regular spear phishing attacks, as the potential rewards are much higher.

Phishing attacks can also be conducted over the phone, a technique known as vishing (voice phishing), or through text messages, known as smishing (SMS phishing). The principles are the same: the attacker impersonates a trusted entity to trick the victim into revealing sensitive information or performing an action that compromises security.

Denial-of-service (DoS) attacks are another common cyber threat. A DoS attack aims to disrupt the availability of a service or resource by overwhelming it with traffic from multiple sources. This can make the service or resource unavailable to legitimate users, causing operational disruptions and potential financial losses.

DoS attacks can be carried out using various techniques, such as flooding a server with requests, sending malformed packets that crash the system, or exploiting vulnerabilities in network protocols. A distributed denial-of-service (DDoS) attack is a DoS attack that uses a network of compromised computers, known as a botnet, to amplify the attack. DDoS attacks can be very difficult to defend against, as the traffic comes from multiple sources and can be difficult to distinguish from legitimate traffic.

Man-in-the-middle (MitM) attacks are another type of cyber threat that involves intercepting and potentially altering communications between two parties without their knowledge. In a MitM attack, the attacker secretly relays and possibly alters the communication between two parties who believe they are directly communicating with each other.

MitM attacks can be used to eavesdrop on communications, steal sensitive information, or even inject malicious code into the communication stream. These attacks can be carried out on various communication channels, such as email, instant messaging, or even web browsing.

SQL injection is a type of attack that targets web applications that use databases. In a SQL injection attack, the attacker inserts malicious SQL code into an input field on a web form, such as a search box or a login form. If the web application is not properly secured, the malicious code can be executed by the database, allowing the attacker to gain unauthorized access to the data, modify it, or even delete it.

Cross-site scripting (XSS) is another type of attack that targets web applications. In an XSS attack, the attacker injects malicious scripts into web pages viewed by other users. When a user visits the compromised web page, the malicious script is executed in their browser, allowing the attacker to steal their cookies, redirect them to a malicious website, or even take control of their browser session.

Zero-day exploits are vulnerabilities in software or hardware that are unknown to the vendor or for which no patch is yet available. These vulnerabilities can be exploited by attackers to gain unauthorized access to systems or data. Zero-day exploits are particularly dangerous because there is no defense against them until a patch is released.

These are just a few examples of the many cyber threats that businesses face. The specific threats that your organization is most likely to encounter will depend on a variety of factors, including your industry, your size, your technology infrastructure, and the value of your digital assets.

Now that we've covered some of the most common cyber threats, let's discuss the attack vectors used to deliver them. An attack vector is the path or means by which an attacker gains access to a system or network. Understanding these attack vectors is crucial for developing effective defenses.

One of the most common attack vectors is email. Email is a ubiquitous communication tool used by businesses of all sizes. It's also a popular target for cybercriminals. Attackers can use email to deliver malware, such as viruses, worms, or Trojans, through malicious attachments or links. They can also use email to conduct phishing attacks, tricking users into divulging sensitive information or performing actions that compromise security.

Another common attack vector is compromised websites. Attackers can compromise legitimate websites and inject them with malicious code. When a user visits the compromised website, the malicious code is executed in their browser, potentially infecting their system with malware or redirecting them to a malicious website.

Removable media, such as USB drives, can also be used as an attack vector. Attackers can infect removable media with malware and then leave them in public places, hoping that someone will pick them up and plug them into their computer. When the infected media is connected to a computer, the malware can automatically install itself on the system.

Social engineering is another powerful attack vector. Social engineering involves manipulating individuals into divulging sensitive information or performing actions that compromise security. This can be done through various means, such as phone calls, emails, text messages, or even in-person interactions. Social engineering attacks exploit human psychology rather than technical vulnerabilities, making them particularly difficult to defend against.

Unpatched software is another common attack vector. Software vulnerabilities are constantly being discovered, and vendors regularly release patches to fix them. However, if users don't install these patches promptly, their systems remain vulnerable to attack. Attackers can exploit these unpatched vulnerabilities to gain unauthorized access to systems or data.

Weak passwords are also a significant attack vector. Many users choose weak passwords that are easy to guess or crack. Attackers can use various techniques, such as brute-force attacks or dictionary attacks, to guess weak passwords and gain unauthorized access to accounts.

Insider threats are another important attack vector to consider. Insider threats are security risks that originate from within the organization. These can be malicious insiders who intentionally seek to harm the organization, or they can be negligent employees who unintentionally compromise security through their actions.

These are just a few examples of the many attack vectors that cybercriminals can use to compromise systems and data. The specific attack vectors that your organization is most vulnerable to will depend on a variety of factors, including your technology infrastructure, your security practices, and the behavior of your employees.

Understanding the various cyber threats and attack vectors is essential for developing a robust cybersecurity strategy. By knowing what you're up against, you can better assess your vulnerabilities, prioritize your security efforts, and implement appropriate controls to mitigate the risks. It's important to remember that the cybersecurity landscape is constantly evolving, with new threats and attack vectors emerging all the time. Staying informed about the latest threats and trends is crucial for maintaining a strong security posture. As a manager, you don't need to be a technical expert, but you do need to have a basic understanding of the threats your organization faces and the measures that can be taken to protect it. This knowledge will enable you to make informed decisions about cybersecurity, allocate resources effectively, and foster a culture of security awareness among your employees. The threat landscape may be complex and daunting, but with the right knowledge and a proactive approach, businesses can navigate these digital dangers and emerge stronger and more resilient.

CHAPTER FOUR: Assessing Your Cybersecurity Risk

Having identified your digital assets and gained an understanding of the common cyber threats and attack vectors, the next crucial step is to assess your organization's specific cybersecurity risk. This process involves evaluating the likelihood and potential impact of various cyber threats materializing against your specific digital assets and vulnerabilities. It's about understanding your unique risk profile, which is shaped by factors such as your industry, the type of data you handle, your technology infrastructure, and your overall security posture.

Risk assessment is not a one-size-fits-all exercise. What constitutes an acceptable level of risk for one organization may be completely unacceptable for another. A small online retailer with a limited customer base and no sensitive data will have a very different risk profile than a large financial institution that handles millions of transactions and stores vast amounts of highly sensitive customer data. Therefore, it's essential to tailor your risk assessment to your specific business context.

The first step in assessing your cybersecurity risk is to identify the potential threats that are most relevant to your organization. While it's important to be aware of the full spectrum of cyber threats, not all threats are equally likely to target your business. For example, a company that operates in the defense industry is more likely to be targeted by state-sponsored actors than a small local business. Similarly, a company that handles large volumes of credit card data is more likely to be targeted by financially motivated cybercriminals.

To identify the most relevant threats, you can start by considering your industry and the types of attacks that are common in your sector. Industry associations, government agencies, and cybersecurity firms often publish reports and threat intelligence that can provide valuable insights into the specific threats facing your industry. You can also analyze your own historical data on security incidents to identify any patterns or trends.

Once you have identified the potential threats, the next step is to assess your vulnerabilities. Vulnerabilities are weaknesses in your systems, networks, or processes that could be exploited by cyber threats. These can be technical vulnerabilities, such as unpatched software or misconfigured firewalls, or they can be non-technical vulnerabilities, such as a lack of security awareness among employees or inadequate physical security controls.

To assess your vulnerabilities, you can use a variety of techniques, including vulnerability scanning, penetration testing, and security audits. Vulnerability scanning involves using automated tools to scan your systems and networks for known vulnerabilities. Penetration testing involves simulating a cyberattack to identify weaknesses in your defenses. Security audits involve reviewing your security policies, procedures, and controls to identify any gaps or weaknesses.

It's important to note that vulnerability assessment is not a one-time activity. New vulnerabilities are constantly being discovered, and your systems and networks are constantly changing. Therefore, it's essential to conduct regular vulnerability assessments to ensure that your defenses are up-to-date.

Once you have identified your threats and vulnerabilities, the next step is to assess the likelihood of each threat exploiting a specific vulnerability. This involves considering factors such as the attacker's motivation, capabilities, and resources, as well as the effectiveness of your existing security controls.

For example, a state-sponsored actor with advanced capabilities and resources is more likely to successfully exploit a complex vulnerability than a script kiddie with limited skills and resources. Similarly, a vulnerability that is protected by multiple layers of security controls is less likely to be exploited than a vulnerability that is not protected at all.

Assessing the likelihood of a threat exploiting a vulnerability is often a subjective exercise, as it involves making judgments based on incomplete information. However, there are various frameworks and methodologies that can help you make more informed assessments. For example, you can use a qualitative scale, such as low, medium, and high, or a quantitative scale, such as a numerical score from 1 to 10, to rate the likelihood of each threat-vulnerability pair.

Once you have assessed the likelihood, the next step is to assess the potential impact of each threat-vulnerability pair. This involves considering the potential consequences if a particular threat were to successfully exploit a specific vulnerability. The impact could be financial, operational, reputational, or legal.

For example, a successful ransomware attack could lead to significant financial losses due to ransom payments, business interruption, and data recovery costs. It could also damage your reputation and lead to legal liabilities if customer data is compromised.

To assess the potential impact, you can use a similar approach as for assessing likelihood. You can use a qualitative scale, such as low, medium, and high, or a quantitative scale, such as a numerical score, to rate the potential impact of each threat-vulnerability pair.

Once you have assessed the likelihood and potential impact of each threat-vulnerability pair, you can combine these assessments to determine the overall risk level. This is often done using a risk matrix, which is a simple tool that plots likelihood against impact to visualize the risk level.

For example, a threat-vulnerability pair with a high likelihood and a high impact would be considered a high risk, while a threat-vulnerability pair with a low likelihood and a low impact would be considered a low risk.

The risk matrix helps you prioritize your security efforts by identifying the highest-risk areas that require immediate attention.

You can then focus your resources on mitigating these high-risk areas first, before addressing lower-risk areas.

It's important to note that risk assessment is not a static process. Your risk landscape is constantly changing as new threats emerge, new vulnerabilities are discovered, and your business evolves. Therefore, it's essential to regularly review and update your risk assessment to ensure that it remains relevant and accurate.

One way to ensure that your risk assessment stays current is to incorporate it into your overall risk management process. This involves establishing a framework for identifying, assessing, mitigating, and monitoring risks on an ongoing basis. It also involves assigning roles and responsibilities for risk management and establishing clear communication channels to ensure that everyone is aware of their responsibilities.

Another important aspect of risk assessment is to involve key stakeholders from across the organization. Cybersecurity is not just an IT issue; it's a business issue that affects everyone. Therefore, it's essential to involve business unit leaders, legal counsel, human resources, and other key stakeholders in the risk assessment process. This helps ensure that the risk assessment is comprehensive and that it accurately reflects the organization's overall risk tolerance.

Once you have completed your risk assessment, the next step is to develop a risk mitigation strategy. This involves identifying and implementing controls to reduce the likelihood or impact of the identified risks. Controls can be technical, such as firewalls and intrusion detection systems, or they can be non-technical, such as security policies and employee training.

When selecting controls, it's important to consider their effectiveness, cost, and impact on business operations. You want to choose controls that are effective at mitigating the identified risks, but you also want to ensure that they are cost-effective and that they don't unduly hinder your business operations.

It's also important to prioritize your controls based on the risk level. You should focus on implementing controls for high-risk areas first, before addressing lower-risk areas. This ensures that you are allocating your resources effectively and that you are addressing the most critical risks first.

Once you have implemented your controls, it's important to monitor their effectiveness on an ongoing basis. This involves regularly testing your controls to ensure that they are working as intended and that they are still effective against the latest threats.

Monitoring can involve various techniques, such as vulnerability scanning, penetration testing, and security audits. It can also involve monitoring security logs and alerts to identify any potential security incidents.

If you find that your controls are not effective, you need to take corrective action. This may involve modifying existing controls, implementing new controls, or even accepting the risk if it is deemed to be within your organization's risk tolerance.

Risk assessment is a critical component of any cybersecurity program. It helps you understand your unique risk profile, prioritize your security efforts, and allocate resources effectively. By regularly assessing your risks and implementing appropriate controls, you can significantly reduce your exposure to cyber threats and protect your valuable digital assets.

It's important to remember that risk assessment is not a one-time exercise. It's an ongoing process that needs to be integrated into your overall risk management framework. By regularly reviewing and updating your risk assessment, you can ensure that your security posture remains strong and that you are prepared to address the ever-evolving cyber threat landscape.

In addition to the technical aspects of risk assessment, it's also important to consider the human element. Your employees play a critical role in your overall security posture. They can be your strongest defense against cyber threats, or they can be your weakest link.

Security awareness training is a crucial component of any risk mitigation strategy. By educating your employees about the various cyber threats they may encounter and how to recognize and respond to them, you can significantly reduce the likelihood of a successful attack.

Security awareness training should cover topics such as phishing, malware, social engineering, and password security. It should also be tailored to your specific industry and the types of threats that your employees are most likely to encounter.

In addition to training, it's also important to foster a culture of security awareness within your organization. This involves creating a shared sense of responsibility for security and encouraging employees to report any suspicious activity or potential security incidents.

Another important aspect of risk assessment is to consider the potential impact of a security incident on your business continuity. Business continuity planning is the process of developing a plan to ensure that your critical business operations can continue in the event of a major disruption, such as a natural disaster or a cyberattack.

Your risk assessment should inform your business continuity plan by identifying the potential impact of various security incidents on your critical business operations. This helps you prioritize your recovery efforts and ensure that you can restore your most critical operations first.

Your business continuity plan should also include procedures for responding to a security incident. This involves establishing clear roles and responsibilities, communication protocols, and escalation procedures. It also involves regularly testing your plan to ensure that it is effective and that everyone knows what to do in the event of an incident.

Third-party risk management is another important consideration in your overall risk assessment. As businesses increasingly rely on external vendors and service providers, it's essential to assess the security risks associated with these third parties.

Your risk assessment should include an evaluation of the security practices of your third-party vendors, particularly those that handle sensitive data or have access to your systems. This may involve reviewing their security policies, conducting security audits, or requiring them to provide evidence of their security certifications.

You should also have a process in place for monitoring the security performance of your third-party vendors on an ongoing basis. This may involve requiring them to report any security incidents or vulnerabilities that they discover, or it may involve conducting regular security assessments of their systems.

Finally, it's important to remember that risk assessment is not just about identifying risks; it's also about making informed decisions about how to manage those risks. Not all risks can be eliminated, and not all risks should be eliminated.

Some risks may be deemed to be within your organization's risk tolerance, meaning that the potential impact of the risk is outweighed by the cost or complexity of mitigating it. In these cases, it may be acceptable to simply accept the risk and monitor it on an ongoing basis.

Other risks may be transferred to a third party, such as through the purchase of cybersecurity insurance. Cybersecurity insurance can help mitigate the financial impact of a security incident, such as the cost of data recovery, legal fees, and regulatory fines.

Ultimately, the goal of risk assessment is to provide you with the information you need to make informed decisions about how to manage your cybersecurity risks. By understanding your unique risk profile, prioritizing your security efforts, and implementing appropriate controls, you can significantly reduce your exposure to cyber threats and protect your valuable digital assets. The process of risk assessment is a journey, not a destination. It requires continuous effort, vigilance, and adaptation. But by embracing this process, businesses can build a more resilient and secure future, better prepared to withstand the challenges of the digital age. Through careful analysis and strategic planning, organizations can transform their approach to cybersecurity from a reactive stance to a proactive posture, effectively safeguarding their operations and maintaining the trust of their stakeholders.

CHAPTER FIVE: Building a Cybersecurity Strategy

Having assessed your organization's cybersecurity risk in the previous chapter, you now possess a clearer understanding of your vulnerabilities, the potential threats you face, and the possible impact of a successful cyberattack. The next logical step is to use this knowledge to build a comprehensive cybersecurity strategy. This strategy will serve as your roadmap for protecting your digital assets, mitigating risks, and ensuring the resilience of your business in the face of evolving cyber threats.

A cybersecurity strategy is not just a document; it's a living, breathing framework that guides your organization's security efforts. It's not something you create once and then file away. It needs to be regularly reviewed, updated, and adapted to the changing threat landscape and your evolving business needs.

Building a cybersecurity strategy is not solely an IT function. It requires collaboration and input from across the organization. Business unit leaders, legal counsel, human resources, and other key stakeholders all have a role to play in shaping the strategy. This ensures that the strategy aligns with your overall business objectives and that it addresses the specific security needs of each department.

The first step in building your cybersecurity strategy is to define your security objectives. What are you trying to achieve with your security program? What are your priorities? Your objectives should be specific, measurable, achievable, relevant, and time-bound (SMART).

For example, your objectives might include:

- Protecting sensitive customer data from unauthorized access.

- Ensuring the availability of critical business systems.

- Complying with relevant data protection regulations.

- Minimizing the impact of security incidents.

- Fostering a culture of security awareness among employees.

Your security objectives should be directly linked to your risk assessment. The highest-priority objectives should address the highest-risk areas identified in your risk assessment. For example, if your risk assessment identified a high risk of ransomware attacks, one of your security objectives might be to implement measures to prevent and mitigate the impact of such attacks.

Once you have defined your security objectives, the next step is to identify the appropriate controls and countermeasures to achieve those objectives. Controls are the safeguards you put in place to protect your digital assets and mitigate risks. They can be technical, such as firewalls, intrusion detection systems, and encryption, or they can be non-technical, such as security policies, procedures, and employee training.

When selecting controls, it's important to consider their effectiveness, cost, and impact on business operations. You want to choose controls that are effective at mitigating the identified risks, but you also want to ensure that they are cost-effective and that they don't unduly hinder your business operations.

It's also important to take a layered approach to security. This means implementing multiple layers of controls so that if one control fails, another is there to provide protection. For example, you might have a firewall to protect your network perimeter, intrusion detection systems to monitor for suspicious activity, and antivirus software to protect your endpoints.

Another important principle is the principle of least privilege. This means that users should only have access to the data and systems that they need to perform their jobs. This helps to limit the potential damage that can be caused by a compromised account.

Once you have identified the appropriate controls, you need to develop a plan for implementing them. This plan should include timelines, resource requirements, and responsibilities. It should also include a process for monitoring the effectiveness of the controls and making adjustments as needed.

Implementing controls is not a one-time activity. It's an ongoing process that requires regular review and updates. New threats and vulnerabilities are constantly emerging, and your systems and networks are constantly changing. Therefore, it's essential to regularly assess the effectiveness of your controls and make adjustments as needed to ensure that they remain effective.

In addition to implementing controls, your cybersecurity strategy should also include a plan for responding to security incidents. No matter how well-prepared you are, security incidents can still occur. Having a plan in place to deal with these incidents can minimize the impact and ensure a swift and effective recovery.

Your incident response plan should include procedures for detecting, analyzing, containing, eradicating, and recovering from security incidents. It should also include clear roles and responsibilities, communication protocols, and escalation procedures.

It's important to regularly test your incident response plan to ensure that it is effective and that everyone knows what to do in the event of an incident. This can be done through tabletop exercises, simulations, or even live-fire drills.

Another important component of your cybersecurity strategy is security awareness training. Your employees play a critical role in your overall security posture. They can be your strongest defense against cyber threats, or they can be your weakest link.

Security awareness training should educate your employees about the various cyber threats they may encounter and how to recognize and respond to them. It should cover topics such as phishing, malware, social engineering, and password security.

Training should be tailored to your specific industry and the types of threats that your employees are most likely to encounter. It should also be engaging and interactive to ensure that employees retain the information.

In addition to training, it's important to foster a culture of security awareness within your organization. This involves creating a shared sense of responsibility for security and encouraging employees to report any suspicious activity or potential security incidents.

Your cybersecurity strategy should also address the issue of third-party risk management. As businesses increasingly rely on external vendors and service providers, it's essential to assess the security risks associated with these third parties.

Your strategy should include a process for evaluating the security practices of your third-party vendors, particularly those that handle sensitive data or have access to your systems. This may involve reviewing their security policies, conducting security audits, or requiring them to provide evidence of their security certifications.

You should also have a process in place for monitoring the security performance of your third-party vendors on an ongoing basis. This may involve requiring them to report any security incidents or vulnerabilities that they discover, or it may involve conducting regular security assessments of their systems.

Your cybersecurity strategy should also consider the role of cybersecurity insurance. Cybersecurity insurance can help mitigate the financial impact of a security incident, such as the cost of data recovery, legal fees, and regulatory fines.

When considering cybersecurity insurance, it's important to understand the different types of coverage available and the specific terms and conditions of each policy. You should also assess your organization's specific needs and risk profile to determine the appropriate level of coverage.

Another important aspect of your cybersecurity strategy is to establish a framework for ongoing monitoring and improvement. Cybersecurity is not a static discipline; it's a continuous process of improvement.

Your strategy should include a process for regularly monitoring your security posture, identifying any weaknesses or gaps, and making necessary improvements. This may involve conducting regular vulnerability assessments, penetration tests, and security audits.

It may also involve monitoring security logs and alerts to identify any potential security incidents. You should also stay informed about the latest threats and vulnerabilities and adapt your security controls accordingly.

Your cybersecurity strategy should also include a process for measuring the effectiveness of your security program. This involves establishing metrics and key performance indicators (KPIs) to track your progress and identify areas for improvement.

Metrics and KPIs might include the number of security incidents, the time it takes to detect and respond to incidents, the number of vulnerabilities identified and remediated, and the level of employee security awareness.

Regularly reviewing your metrics and KPIs will help you assess the effectiveness of your security program and make data-driven decisions about where to invest your resources.

Building a cybersecurity strategy is a complex undertaking, but it's essential for protecting your organization from the ever-evolving threat landscape. By defining your security objectives, identifying appropriate controls, developing an incident response plan, and fostering a culture of security awareness, you can significantly reduce your exposure to cyber threats and build a more resilient organization.

Remember, your cybersecurity strategy is not a one-size-fits-all solution. It needs to be tailored to your specific business context, taking into account your industry, your size, your technology infrastructure, and your risk tolerance.

It's also important to remember that your cybersecurity strategy is not a static document. It needs to be regularly reviewed, updated, and adapted to the changing threat landscape and your evolving business needs.

Involving key stakeholders from across the organization is crucial for developing a comprehensive and effective cybersecurity strategy. By working together, you can create a strategy that aligns with your overall business objectives and addresses the specific security needs of each department.

As you develop your cybersecurity strategy, it's also important to consider the broader context of your industry and the regulatory environment. Different industries have different security requirements, and there are a growing number of data protection and privacy regulations that businesses need to comply with.

Your cybersecurity strategy should take into account these industry-specific requirements and regulations, ensuring that your security controls and practices are in line with industry best practices and legal obligations.

Another important consideration is the role of emerging technologies in shaping the cybersecurity landscape. Technologies such as artificial intelligence, machine learning, and the Internet of Things are creating new opportunities for businesses, but they are also introducing new security challenges.

Your cybersecurity strategy should consider the potential impact of these emerging technologies on your security posture and should include plans for addressing any new risks that they may introduce.

Finally, it's important to remember that building a cybersecurity strategy is not just about implementing technical controls. It's also about creating a culture of security awareness within your organization.

This involves fostering a shared sense of responsibility for security, encouraging open communication about security issues, and providing ongoing training and awareness programs. By creating a culture of security awareness, you can empower your employees to be your first line of defense against cyber threats.

A well-crafted cybersecurity strategy should also include a plan for communicating about security incidents, both internally and externally. In the event of a breach or other security incident, it's important to have a clear and consistent communication plan in place.

This plan should outline who needs to be informed about the incident, what information should be shared, and how the communication should be handled. It should also include procedures for communicating with customers, partners, regulators, and the media, if necessary.

Transparent and timely communication can help to minimize the damage to your reputation and maintain the trust of your stakeholders.

Your cybersecurity strategy should also address the issue of data governance. Data governance is the process of managing the availability, usability, integrity, and security of the data used in an organization.

A strong data governance framework can help to ensure that data is properly classified, handled, and protected throughout its lifecycle. It can also help to ensure compliance with data protection regulations and industry best practices.

Your data governance framework should include policies and procedures for data classification, data access control, data retention, and data disposal. It should also define roles and responsibilities for data management and establish a process for monitoring compliance with data governance policies.

Another important aspect of your cybersecurity strategy is to establish a process for continuous improvement. The cybersecurity landscape is constantly evolving, and your security program needs to evolve with it.

This involves regularly reviewing your security controls, policies, and procedures to ensure that they are still effective and relevant. It also involves staying informed about the latest threats and vulnerabilities and adapting your security posture accordingly.

Continuous improvement can be achieved through various means, such as conducting regular security assessments, participating in industry forums and information-sharing groups, and engaging with external security experts.

By embracing a culture of continuous improvement, you can ensure that your cybersecurity program remains strong and that you are prepared to address the ever-evolving threat landscape.

Building a cybersecurity strategy is a critical undertaking for any organization operating in today's digital environment. It's a process that requires careful planning, collaboration, and ongoing attention. By taking a comprehensive and proactive approach to cybersecurity, you can protect your organization's digital assets, maintain the trust of your customers and partners, and ensure your continued success in the digital age. Your strategy is the blueprint that will guide your efforts, ensuring that every action taken is purposeful and contributes to the overarching goal of a secure and resilient organization. It's a commitment to safeguarding not just data and systems, but the very future of your business in an interconnected world.

CHAPTER SIX: Implementing a Security Framework

With your cybersecurity strategy defined, outlining your objectives, controls, and response plans, the next crucial step is to put that strategy into action. This is where a security framework comes into play. A security framework provides a structured approach to implementing and managing your cybersecurity program. It's like a blueprint that helps you build a solid and reliable security foundation for your organization.

Think of a security framework as a set of guidelines, best practices, and standards that help you organize and prioritize your security efforts. It provides a common language and a systematic way to address cybersecurity risks. Instead of a haphazard, piecemeal approach to security, a framework helps you build a comprehensive and cohesive program that aligns with your business objectives and risk tolerance.

There are several recognized security frameworks available, each with its own strengths and focus areas. Some of the most widely adopted frameworks include the NIST Cybersecurity Framework (CSF), ISO 27001/27002, and the CIS Controls. While these frameworks differ in their specific requirements and structure, they all share a common goal: to help organizations improve their cybersecurity posture.

The NIST Cybersecurity Framework (CSF) was developed by the National Institute of Standards and Technology (NIST) in the United States. It was initially designed for critical infrastructure organizations but has since been adopted by businesses of all sizes and across various industries. The NIST CSF is a voluntary framework that provides a set of guidelines and best practices for managing cybersecurity risk.

The NIST CSF is organized around five core functions: Identify, Protect, Detect, Respond, and Recover. These functions represent the key stages of a comprehensive cybersecurity program. The Identify function focuses on understanding your business context, identifying your digital assets, and assessing your cybersecurity risks. The Protect function focuses on implementing safeguards to protect your assets and mitigate risks. The Detect function focuses on implementing measures to identify security incidents. The Respond function focuses on having a plan in place to respond to security incidents. The Recover function focuses on having a plan in place to restore your operations after a security incident.

Each of these core functions is further broken down into categories and subcategories, which provide more specific guidance on the activities and outcomes associated with each function. For example, under the Protect function, there are categories such as Access Control, Awareness and Training, and Data Security. Each of these categories has subcategories that provide more detailed guidance.

The NIST CSF also includes implementation tiers, which describe the degree to which an organization's cybersecurity risk management practices exhibit the characteristics defined in the framework. These tiers range from Tier 1 (Partial) to Tier 4 (Adaptive) and provide a way for organizations to measure their current level of cybersecurity maturity and set goals for improvement.

ISO 27001/27002 is an international standard for information security management developed by the International Organization for Standardization (ISO) and the International Electrotechnical Commission (IEC). ISO 27001 provides a framework for establishing, implementing, maintaining, and continually improving an Information Security Management System (ISMS). An ISMS is a systematic approach to managing sensitive company information so that it remains secure. It includes people, processes, and IT systems by applying a risk management process.

ISO 27002 provides a set of best practices for information security controls. It covers a wide range of security topics, including security policy, access control, cryptography, physical security, and incident management. ISO 27001 is a certifiable standard, meaning that organizations can obtain independent certification to demonstrate their compliance with the standard.

The CIS Controls, developed by the Center for Internet Security (CIS), are a prioritized set of actions that collectively form a defense-in-depth set of best practices that mitigate the most common attacks against systems and networks. The CIS Controls are organized into 20 controls, each of which addresses a specific area of cybersecurity. These controls are prioritized based on their effectiveness in mitigating real-world threats.

The CIS Controls are designed to be implementable and measurable. They provide specific guidance on what organizations should do to protect themselves from cyber threats. The CIS Controls are also mapped to other security frameworks, such as the NIST CSF and ISO 27001/27002, making it easier for organizations to use them in conjunction with other frameworks.

Choosing the right security framework for your organization depends on several factors, including your industry, your size, your regulatory requirements, and your risk tolerance. You may choose to adopt a single framework, or you may choose to use elements from multiple frameworks to create a customized approach that best meets your needs.

For example, a small business with limited resources might choose to start with the CIS Controls, as they provide a prioritized set of actions that can be implemented relatively easily. A larger organization with more complex security requirements might choose to adopt the NIST CSF or ISO 27001/27002, as these frameworks provide a more comprehensive approach to managing cybersecurity risk.

Regardless of which framework you choose, the key is to use it as a guide to help you implement and manage your cybersecurity program. It's not about blindly following a set of rules; it's about using the framework as a tool to help you make informed decisions about your security posture.

Once you have selected a framework, the next step is to adapt it to your specific business context. This involves tailoring the framework's guidelines and best practices to your organization's unique needs and circumstances.

For example, if you choose to adopt the NIST CSF, you would start by assessing your current cybersecurity posture against the framework's five core functions. This involves identifying your existing controls and practices and comparing them to the framework's categories and subcategories.

This gap analysis will help you identify areas where your current practices align with the framework and areas where you need to make improvements. You can then use this information to prioritize your security efforts and develop a roadmap for implementing the framework.

It's important to remember that implementing a security framework is not a one-time project; it's an ongoing process. As your business evolves and the threat landscape changes, you will need to regularly review and update your implementation of the framework to ensure that it remains relevant and effective.

One of the key benefits of using a security framework is that it provides a common language for discussing cybersecurity within your organization. This helps to ensure that everyone is on the same page and that security is integrated into all aspects of your business operations.

A security framework also helps you demonstrate your commitment to cybersecurity to your customers, partners, and regulators. By adopting a recognized framework, you are showing that you are taking cybersecurity seriously and that you have implemented a systematic approach to managing your risks.

Implementing a security framework can also help you improve your overall security posture. By following the framework's guidelines and best practices, you can identify and address weaknesses in your defenses, reduce your exposure to cyber threats, and improve your ability to respond to and recover from security incidents.

Another important aspect of implementing a security framework is to establish clear roles and responsibilities for cybersecurity within your organization. This involves defining who is responsible for each aspect of your security program, from developing policies and procedures to monitoring security logs and responding to incidents.

Having clear roles and responsibilities helps to ensure that everyone knows what is expected of them and that there is accountability for security throughout the organization. It also helps to prevent security tasks from falling through the cracks or being duplicated.

As you implement your chosen security framework, it's important to document your policies, procedures, and controls. This documentation serves as a reference guide for your employees and helps to ensure that your security practices are consistently applied.

Documentation should include your overall security policy, which outlines your organization's approach to cybersecurity and sets the tone for your security program. It should also include specific procedures for implementing and managing your security controls, as well as guidelines for responding to security incidents.

Regularly reviewing and updating your documentation is crucial to ensure that it remains accurate and relevant. As your security program evolves and your business changes, your documentation should be updated to reflect these changes.

Another important aspect of implementing a security framework is to establish a process for monitoring and measuring the effectiveness of your security program. This involves establishing metrics and key performance indicators (KPIs) to track your progress and identify areas for improvement.

Metrics and KPIs might include the number of security incidents, the time it takes to detect and respond to incidents, the number of vulnerabilities identified and remediated, and the level of employee security awareness.

Regularly reviewing your metrics and KPIs will help you assess the effectiveness of your security program and make data-driven decisions about where to invest your resources. It also helps you demonstrate the value of your security program to your organization's leadership and stakeholders.

Implementing a security framework also requires ongoing training and awareness for your employees. Your employees play a critical role in your overall security posture, and they need to be aware of the threats they face and the role they play in protecting your organization.

Security awareness training should be tailored to your specific industry and the types of threats that your employees are most likely to encounter. It should cover topics such as phishing, malware, social engineering, and password security. Training should be engaging, interactive, and regularly reinforced to ensure that employees retain the information and apply it to their daily work.

In addition to formal training, it's important to foster a culture of security awareness within your organization. This involves creating a shared sense of responsibility for security, encouraging open communication about security issues, and recognizing and rewarding employees who demonstrate good security practices.

As you implement your security framework, it's also important to consider how you will integrate it with your existing business processes. Security should not be seen as a separate function; it should be embedded in all aspects of your operations.

For example, you should integrate security considerations into your software development lifecycle, your procurement process, and your change management process. This helps to ensure that security is considered from the outset and that it is not an afterthought.

Integrating security into your business processes also helps to ensure that security is not seen as a barrier to innovation or efficiency. By taking a proactive approach to security, you can enable your business to operate more securely and efficiently.

Implementing a security framework can seem like a daunting task, but it's important to remember that it's a journey, not a destination. You don't have to implement everything at once. You can start small, focusing on the highest-priority areas first, and gradually expand your implementation over time.

It's also important to remember that you don't have to do it alone. There are many resources available to help you implement a security framework, including consultants, vendors, and industry associations. You can also learn from the experiences of other organizations that have implemented similar frameworks.

By taking a structured and systematic approach to implementing a security framework, you can significantly improve your organization's cybersecurity posture. You can reduce your exposure to cyber threats, improve your ability to respond to and recover from security incidents, and demonstrate your commitment to cybersecurity to your customers, partners, and regulators.

A security framework provides a roadmap for building a strong and resilient security program. It helps you organize your security efforts, prioritize your investments, and ensure that you are taking a comprehensive and proactive approach to managing your cybersecurity risks. While the specific steps involved in implementing a framework will vary depending on the framework you choose and your organization's unique needs, the overall process remains the same. It's about understanding your risks, implementing appropriate controls, monitoring your effectiveness, and continuously improving your security posture. This ongoing commitment to security, guided by a well-chosen framework, will position your organization to navigate the complex cybersecurity landscape with greater confidence and resilience. It is a strategic investment in the long-term health and success of your business, ensuring that you are well-prepared to meet the challenges of today and the uncertainties of tomorrow.

CHAPTER SEVEN: Data Protection and Privacy Regulations

In the preceding chapters, we've explored the foundational elements of building a robust cybersecurity posture: understanding the threat landscape, identifying your digital assets, assessing your risks, formulating a strategy, and implementing a security framework. Now, we turn our attention to a critical aspect of cybersecurity that has gained increasing prominence in recent years: data protection and privacy regulations. These regulations are not just legal requirements; they represent a fundamental shift in how businesses must approach the handling of personal data. They are a direct response to the growing concerns about the privacy implications of the digital age, and they have far-reaching consequences for businesses of all sizes and across all industries.

As a manager, you may not be a legal expert, but you need to have a solid understanding of the key data protection and privacy regulations that affect your business. Failure to comply with these regulations can result in significant penalties, including hefty fines, reputational damage, and loss of customer trust. More importantly, complying with these regulations is not just about avoiding penalties; it's about demonstrating your commitment to protecting the privacy of your customers, employees, and partners.

The landscape of data protection and privacy regulations is complex and constantly evolving. New laws and regulations are being introduced around the world, each with its own set of requirements and enforcement mechanisms. However, there are some common themes and principles that underpin most of these regulations.

One of the most significant and influential data protection regulations is the General Data Protection Regulation (GDPR), which came into effect in the European Union in May 2018. The GDPR is a comprehensive privacy law that applies to any organization that processes the personal data of individuals in the

EU, regardless of where the organization is located. This means that even if your business is not based in the EU, if you offer goods or services to individuals in the EU or monitor their behavior, you are subject to the GDPR.

The GDPR introduced several key principles for the processing of personal data, including lawfulness, fairness, and transparency; purpose limitation; data minimization; accuracy; storage limitation; integrity and confidentiality; and accountability. These principles are designed to ensure that personal data is processed in a way that respects the rights and freedoms of individuals.

Under the GDPR, personal data is defined broadly as any information relating to an identified or identifiable natural person. This includes not only obvious identifiers such as name, address, and identification number but also online identifiers such as IP address and cookie identifiers.

The GDPR also introduced several new rights for individuals, including the right to access their personal data, the right to rectify inaccurate data, the right to erasure (also known as the "right to be forgotten"), the right to restrict processing, the right to data portability, and the right to object to processing.

One of the most significant aspects of the GDPR is the requirement for organizations to obtain explicit consent from individuals before processing their personal data, unless another lawful basis for processing applies. Consent must be freely given, specific, informed, and unambiguous. This means that organizations can no longer rely on pre-ticked boxes or opt-out mechanisms to obtain consent.

The GDPR also introduced the concept of "data protection by design and by default." This means that organizations must consider data protection and privacy issues at the design stage of any new product or service, and they must implement appropriate technical and organizational measures to ensure that, by default, only personal data that is necessary for each specific purpose is processed.

Another important aspect of the GDPR is the requirement for organizations to appoint a Data Protection Officer (DPO) in certain circumstances. A DPO is responsible for overseeing an organization's data protection strategy and ensuring compliance with the GDPR. You need to appoint a DPO if your core activities involve regular and systematic monitoring of data subjects on a large scale, or if you process special categories of data on a large scale, such as health data or data relating to criminal convictions.

The GDPR also introduced strict requirements for reporting data breaches. Organizations must report certain types of data breaches to the relevant supervisory authority within 72 hours of becoming aware of the breach. In some cases, they must also notify the affected individuals without undue delay.

The penalties for non-compliance with the GDPR are severe. Organizations can be fined up to €20 million or 4% of their annual global turnover, whichever is higher, for the most serious infringements.

While the GDPR is an EU regulation, its impact has been felt globally. Many countries around the world have introduced or are in the process of introducing similar data protection laws, often modeled on the GDPR. This trend towards stronger data protection regulations is sometimes referred to as the "Brussels effect," as it reflects the influence of EU regulations on global standards.

In the United States, there is no single, comprehensive federal law regulating the collection and use of personal data. Instead, there is a patchwork of federal and state laws that address specific aspects of data privacy. However, this landscape is rapidly changing, with several states introducing comprehensive privacy laws in recent years.

One of the most significant state-level privacy laws in the US is the California Consumer Privacy Act (CCPA), which came into effect in January 2020. The CCPA applies to businesses that collect personal information from California residents and meet certain thresholds, such as having annual gross revenues in excess of $25 million, buying, receiving, or selling the personal information of 50,000 or more California consumers, households, or devices, or deriving 50% or more of their annual revenues from selling California consumers' personal information.

The CCPA grants California consumers several new rights, including the right to know what personal information is being collected about them, the right to know whether their personal information is sold or disclosed and to whom, the right to say no to the sale of their personal information, the right to access their personal information, and the right to equal service and price, even if they exercise their privacy rights.

The CCPA also requires businesses to provide notice to consumers at or before the point of collection, informing them of the categories of personal information to be collected and the purposes for which the information will be used. Businesses must also implement reasonable security procedures and practices to protect personal information from unauthorized access, destruction, use, modification, or disclosure.

The penalties for non-compliance with the CCPA can be significant. The California Attorney General can bring civil actions against businesses that violate the CCPA, with fines of up to $2,500 per violation or $7,500 per intentional violation. The CCPA also provides a private right of action for consumers whose personal information is subject to certain types of data breaches, with statutory damages ranging from $100 to $750 per consumer per incident, or actual damages, whichever is greater.

Following the enactment of the CCPA, several other states have introduced or are considering similar comprehensive privacy laws. For example, the Virginia Consumer Data Protection Act (CDPA) was signed into law in March 2021 and will take effect on January 1, 2023. The CDPA shares some similarities with the CCPA and the GDPR but also has some unique provisions.

The CDPA applies to businesses that conduct business in Virginia or produce products or services that are targeted to residents of

Virginia and that, during a calendar year, control or process the personal data of at least 100,000 Virginia consumers or control or process the personal data of at least 25,000 Virginia consumers and derive over 50% of their gross revenue from the sale of personal data.

The CDPA grants Virginia consumers several rights, including the right to confirm whether a controller is processing their personal data and to access that data, the right to correct inaccuracies in their personal data, the right to delete their personal data, the right to obtain a copy of their personal data in a portable and readily usable format, and the right to opt out of the processing of their personal data for purposes of targeted advertising, the sale of personal data, or profiling in furtherance of decisions that produce legal or similarly significant effects concerning the consumer.

The CDPA requires controllers to provide consumers with a reasonably accessible, clear, and meaningful privacy notice that includes information such as the categories of personal data processed by the controller, the purpose for processing personal data, how consumers may exercise their rights, and the categories of personal data that the controller shares with third parties.

The CDPA also requires controllers to conduct and document data protection assessments for certain processing activities, such as the processing of personal data for purposes of targeted advertising, the sale of personal data, the processing of sensitive data, and any processing activities involving personal data that present a heightened risk of harm to consumers.

The CDPA does not provide a private right of action. Instead, the Virginia Attorney General has exclusive authority to enforce the CDPA. Controllers that violate the CDPA may be subject to an injunction and may be liable for civil penalties of up to $7,500 per violation.

In addition to the CCPA and the CDPA, several other states, such as New York, Washington, and Illinois, have considered or are considering comprehensive privacy legislation. This trend towards stronger state-level privacy laws is likely to continue, creating an increasingly complex regulatory landscape for businesses that operate across multiple states.

At the federal level, there have been numerous attempts to enact a comprehensive federal privacy law, but so far, none have been successful. However, there is growing momentum for federal privacy legislation, and it is possible that a federal law could be enacted in the coming years. A federal privacy law could potentially preempt some or all state privacy laws, creating a more uniform national standard for data protection.

In addition to these comprehensive privacy laws, there are several sector-specific privacy laws in the US that address the collection and use of personal data in specific industries or contexts. For example, the Health Insurance Portability and Accountability Act (HIPAA) regulates the privacy and security of health information held by covered entities, such as healthcare providers and health plans. The Gramm-Leach-Bliley Act (GLBA) regulates the privacy and security of financial information held by financial institutions. The Children's Online Privacy Protection Act (COPPA) regulates the online collection of personal information from children under the age of 13.

Complying with these data protection and privacy regulations requires a comprehensive and proactive approach. It's not just about implementing technical security measures; it's about embedding data protection and privacy into your organization's culture and processes.

One of the first steps in ensuring compliance is to conduct a data mapping exercise. This involves identifying all the personal data that your organization collects, processes, stores, and shares. You need to understand what data you have, where it comes from, where it goes, and how it is used.

Once you have mapped your data, you need to assess your current practices against the requirements of the relevant regulations. This involves reviewing your policies, procedures, and contracts to ensure that they are in line with the regulations. You may need to update your privacy notices, obtain consent from individuals for processing their data, and implement mechanisms for individuals to exercise their rights.

You also need to implement appropriate technical and organizational measures to protect personal data. This includes implementing access controls, encryption, and other security measures to prevent unauthorized access, use, disclosure, alteration, or destruction of personal data. You should also regularly test your security measures to ensure that they are effective.

Another important aspect of compliance is to provide training to your employees on data protection and privacy. Your employees need to understand their obligations under the regulations and how to handle personal data in a compliant manner. Training should be tailored to the specific roles and responsibilities of your employees and should be regularly updated to reflect changes in the regulations and your organization's practices.

You also need to have a process in place for responding to data breaches. This involves establishing clear procedures for detecting, reporting, and investigating data breaches. You should also have a plan in place for notifying the relevant authorities and affected individuals in the event of a breach, in accordance with the requirements of the regulations.

In addition to complying with existing regulations, it's important to stay informed about new and emerging regulations that may affect your business. The regulatory landscape is constantly evolving, and new laws and regulations are being introduced all the time. You should regularly monitor developments in data protection and privacy law and adapt your practices accordingly.

Complying with data protection and privacy regulations is not just a legal obligation; it's also good for business. By demonstrating your commitment to protecting the privacy of your customers, employees, and partners, you can build trust and enhance your reputation. In today's data-driven economy, trust is a valuable commodity, and organizations that are seen as trustworthy are more likely to succeed.

Data protection and privacy regulations also present an opportunity to improve your data management practices. By understanding what data you have, how it is used, and where it is stored, you can identify opportunities to streamline your processes, reduce costs, and improve efficiency. You can also identify and eliminate unnecessary data collection and processing, reducing your exposure to risk.

Moreover, by implementing strong data protection and privacy practices, you can reduce the risk of data breaches and other security incidents. This can help you avoid the financial and reputational damage that can result from such incidents. By taking a proactive approach to data protection and privacy, you can protect your organization's valuable data assets and maintain the trust of your stakeholders.

The trend towards stronger data protection and privacy regulations is likely to continue in the coming years. As individuals become more aware of their rights and the value of their personal data, they will increasingly demand that organizations take steps to protect their privacy. Regulators are also likely to continue to introduce new laws and regulations to address emerging privacy challenges, such as those posed by artificial intelligence and other new technologies.

To prepare for this future, organizations need to adopt a proactive and comprehensive approach to data protection and privacy. This involves embedding data protection and privacy into your organization's culture, processes, and systems. It also involves staying informed about new and emerging regulations and adapting your practices accordingly.

By taking these steps, you can ensure that your organization is not only compliant with current regulations but also prepared for future developments. You can build a culture of trust and demonstrate your commitment to protecting the privacy of your customers, employees, and partners. In doing so, you can position your organization for success in the data-driven economy of the 21st century.

As a manager, you play a critical role in ensuring that your organization complies with data protection and privacy regulations. You need to understand the key regulations that affect your business and ensure that your team is aware of their obligations. You also need to work with your IT and legal teams to implement appropriate policies, procedures, and technical measures to protect personal data.

By taking a proactive and informed approach to data protection and privacy, you can help your organization navigate the complex regulatory landscape and build a culture of trust. You can protect your organization's valuable data assets, maintain the trust of your stakeholders, and position your organization for success in the digital age. The journey towards strong data protection and privacy is ongoing, requiring continuous effort, vigilance, and adaptation. But by embracing this journey, businesses can build a more resilient, trustworthy, and successful future in an increasingly data-centric world. Through careful planning, implementation, and ongoing management, organizations can transform their approach to data protection and privacy from a compliance burden into a strategic advantage, effectively safeguarding their operations and maintaining the trust of their stakeholders in an interconnected world.

CHAPTER EIGHT: Network Security Fundamentals

In the preceding chapters, we've laid the groundwork for understanding the critical aspects of cybersecurity, from recognizing the threat landscape to implementing security frameworks and navigating the complexities of data protection regulations. Now, we turn our attention to a fundamental pillar of any robust cybersecurity program: network security.

Think of your network as the central nervous system of your organization's digital infrastructure. It's the intricate web of interconnected devices, servers, and systems that enables communication, data sharing, and access to critical applications. Just as the human nervous system requires protection to function properly, your network needs robust security measures to safeguard it from cyber threats.

Network security is the practice of protecting your network and its connected resources from unauthorized access, use, disclosure, disruption, modification, or destruction. It involves implementing a combination of hardware and software controls to create a secure perimeter around your network and to monitor and control traffic flowing in and out of it.

At its core, network security is about controlling access to your network and its resources. You want to ensure that only authorized users and devices can connect to your network and that they can only access the resources they need to perform their jobs. This is achieved through a combination of authentication, authorization, and accounting (AAA) mechanisms.

Authentication is the process of verifying the identity of a user or device attempting to connect to your network. This is typically done using a combination of something you know (such as a password), something you have (such as a smart card or token), and something you are (such as a fingerprint or facial recognition).

Authorization is the process of determining what resources an authenticated user or device is allowed to access. This is typically based on the user's role or job function. For example, a sales representative might be authorized to access the customer relationship management (CRM) system but not the human resources system.

Accounting is the process of tracking and logging network activity. This information can be used to monitor for suspicious activity, investigate security incidents, and audit compliance with security policies.

One of the most fundamental network security controls is the firewall. A firewall is a network security device that monitors and controls incoming and outgoing network traffic based on predetermined security rules. It acts as a barrier between your internal network and the external world, blocking unauthorized access and preventing malicious traffic from entering your network.

Firewalls can be hardware-based, software-based, or a combination of both. Hardware-based firewalls are typically dedicated appliances that are installed at the perimeter of your network. Software-based firewalls are typically installed on individual computers or servers.

Firewalls work by examining network traffic and comparing it to a set of rules. These rules specify which types of traffic are allowed to pass through the firewall and which types are blocked. For example, you might have a rule that allows web traffic to pass through the firewall but blocks all other types of traffic.

Firewalls can be configured to filter traffic based on various criteria, such as source and destination IP addresses, port numbers, and protocols. For example, you might configure your firewall to block all traffic from a specific IP address that is known to be associated with malicious activity.

In addition to traditional firewalls, there are also next-generation firewalls (NGFWs). NGFWs are more advanced firewalls that provide additional security features, such as intrusion prevention, application control, and deep packet inspection.

Intrusion prevention systems (IPS) are network security devices that monitor network traffic for malicious activity and can automatically block or prevent attacks. IPSs use various techniques to detect malicious traffic, such as signature-based detection, anomaly-based detection, and stateful protocol analysis.

Signature-based detection involves comparing network traffic to a database of known attack signatures. When a match is found, the IPS can block the traffic or generate an alert. Anomaly-based detection involves establishing a baseline of normal network activity and then looking for deviations from that baseline. When an anomaly is detected, the IPS can generate an alert or block the traffic.

Stateful protocol analysis involves examining the state of network connections to detect malicious activity. For example, an IPS might detect a SYN flood attack by monitoring the number of open TCP connections.

Application control is a feature of NGFWs that allows you to control which applications are allowed to run on your network. This can help to prevent the spread of malware and other malicious software. Application control works by identifying applications based on their network traffic signatures and then applying policies to allow or block specific applications.

Deep packet inspection (DPI) is a feature of NGFWs that allows you to examine the contents of network packets to detect malicious activity. DPI can be used to identify and block malware, detect data exfiltration attempts, and enforce acceptable use policies.

Another important network security control is the virtual private network (VPN). A VPN is a secure tunnel that allows remote users to connect to your network over the internet. VPNs use encryption to protect data as it travels over the public internet, ensuring that it cannot be intercepted or read by unauthorized parties.

VPNs are commonly used by businesses to allow employees to work remotely while still maintaining secure access to company resources. They can also be used to connect branch offices to a central network, creating a secure wide area network (WAN).

There are two main types of VPNs: remote access VPNs and site-to-site VPNs. Remote access VPNs allow individual users to connect to a network from a remote location. Site-to-site VPNs connect two or more networks together, creating a secure tunnel between them.

VPNs can use various protocols to establish a secure connection, such as IPsec, SSL/TLS, and PPTP. IPsec is a suite of protocols that provide authentication, encryption, and data integrity for IP traffic. SSL/TLS is a protocol that provides encryption for web traffic and is commonly used for secure online transactions. PPTP is an older VPN protocol that is less secure than IPsec or SSL/TLS.

In addition to firewalls and VPNs, another important network security control is network segmentation. Network segmentation involves dividing your network into smaller, isolated segments. This can help to limit the impact of a security breach by preventing an attacker from moving laterally across your network.

Network segmentation can be achieved using various techniques, such as VLANs, subnets, and firewalls. VLANs (virtual local area networks) allow you to logically segment your network into separate broadcast domains, even if the devices are physically connected to the same network switch. Subnets are logical divisions of an IP network that allow you to group devices together based on their location or function.

Firewalls can also be used to segment your network by creating separate security zones. For example, you might have a separate zone for your web servers, your database servers, and your internal users. Firewalls can then be used to control traffic between these zones, limiting access to only what is necessary.

Network segmentation can also help to improve network performance by reducing congestion and improving traffic flow. By isolating different types of traffic, you can prevent one type of traffic from impacting the performance of other types of traffic.

Another important aspect of network security is wireless security. Wireless networks are particularly vulnerable to attack because they broadcast data over the airwaves, making it easier for attackers to intercept and eavesdrop on communications.

To secure your wireless network, you should use strong encryption, such as WPA2 or WPA3. These encryption protocols scramble the data transmitted over your wireless network, making it unreadable to anyone who does not have the correct encryption key.

You should also use a strong password for your wireless network. This password should be different from the password you use for other accounts and should be changed regularly.

In addition to encryption, you should also disable SSID broadcasting. SSID broadcasting is a feature that broadcasts the name of your wireless network to anyone within range. By disabling SSID broadcasting, you can make it more difficult for attackers to find your network.

You should also implement MAC address filtering. MAC address filtering allows you to specify which devices are allowed to connect to your wireless network based on their unique MAC addresses. This can help to prevent unauthorized devices from connecting to your network.

Network access control (NAC) is another important security control that can help to secure your network. NAC is a technology that allows you to control which devices are allowed to connect to your network and what they are allowed to do once they are connected.

NAC works by authenticating devices before they are allowed to connect to the network. This authentication can be based on various factors, such as the device's MAC address, operating system, and installed software.

Once a device is authenticated, NAC can then apply policies to control what the device is allowed to do on the network. For example, you might have a policy that only allows corporate-owned devices to access sensitive data.

NAC can also be used to quarantine devices that do not meet your security requirements. For example, if a device is found to be missing critical security patches, NAC can quarantine the device and prevent it from accessing the network until the patches are installed.

Another important aspect of network security is network monitoring. Network monitoring involves continuously monitoring your network for suspicious activity and potential security incidents. This can be done using various tools, such as intrusion detection systems (IDS), security information and event management (SIEM) systems, and network traffic analyzers.

Intrusion detection systems (IDS) are network security devices that monitor network traffic for malicious activity. Unlike IPS, which can automatically block or prevent attacks, IDS only generate alerts when suspicious activity is detected.

Security information and event management (SIEM) systems are software solutions that collect and analyze security data from various sources, such as firewalls, IDS/IPS, and servers. SIEM systems can help you to identify security incidents, investigate their root cause, and respond to them effectively.

Network traffic analyzers are tools that allow you to capture and analyze network traffic. These tools can be used to troubleshoot network problems, monitor network performance, and detect security incidents.

In addition to these technical controls, it's also important to have strong security policies and procedures in place. These policies should define how your network should be used, who is allowed to access it, and what security measures should be in place.

Your security policies should cover topics such as password management, acceptable use, data classification, and incident response. They should be regularly reviewed and updated to ensure that they remain relevant and effective.

It's also important to provide regular security awareness training to your employees. Your employees are often the first line of defense against cyber attacks, and they need to be aware of the threats they face and how to protect themselves and your organization.

Security awareness training should cover topics such as phishing, malware, social engineering, and password security. It should be tailored to your specific industry and the types of threats that your employees are most likely to encounter.

Network security is a complex and constantly evolving field. New threats and vulnerabilities are emerging all the time, and you need to stay up-to-date on the latest security best practices.

One way to stay informed is to subscribe to security newsletters and blogs. These resources can provide you with valuable information about the latest threats, vulnerabilities, and security technologies.

You can also attend security conferences and workshops. These events provide an opportunity to learn from security experts and network with other professionals in the field.

Another important resource is your vendors. Your firewall, VPN, and other security vendors can provide you with valuable information about their products and how to use them effectively. They can also provide you with support in the event of a security incident.

Network security is a critical component of any cybersecurity program. By implementing the appropriate controls, monitoring your network for suspicious activity, and providing regular security awareness training to your employees, you can significantly reduce your risk of a cyber attack and protect your valuable data and systems. It's an ongoing process that requires constant vigilance and adaptation to the ever-changing threat landscape. As a manager, while you may not be configuring firewalls or setting up VPNs yourself, understanding these fundamentals empowers you to make informed decisions, allocate resources effectively, and foster a security-conscious culture within your organization. This proactive approach to network security is not just about protecting data; it's about ensuring the continued operation and success of your business in an increasingly interconnected world.

CHAPTER NINE: Endpoint Protection: Securing Devices

In our journey through the intricacies of cybersecurity, we've fortified the network perimeter, established robust security frameworks, and navigated the regulatory landscape of data protection. Now, we arrive at another critical line of defense: the endpoints. In the context of cybersecurity, endpoints are the individual devices that connect to your network, such as laptops, desktops, smartphones, tablets, servers, and even Internet of Things (IoT) devices. They are the entry points to your network, and if not properly secured, they can be exploited by cybercriminals to gain access to your valuable data and systems.

Think of endpoints as the doors and windows of your digital house. You can have the strongest locks on your front door, but if you leave a window open, it becomes an easy entry point for intruders. Similarly, you can have a robust firewall protecting your network, but if your endpoints are not secured, they can be compromised, providing a gateway for attackers to bypass your network defenses.

Endpoint protection is the practice of securing these entry points to your network. It involves implementing a combination of technical controls, policies, and procedures to protect endpoints from cyber threats. The goal is to prevent, detect, and respond to attacks that target endpoints, ensuring that they cannot be used as a stepping stone to compromise your network or steal your data.

The importance of endpoint protection has grown significantly in recent years, driven by several factors. First, the number of endpoints has exploded with the rise of mobile devices, remote work, and the Internet of Things. This has dramatically expanded the attack surface, providing more opportunities for cybercriminals to exploit vulnerabilities.

Second, endpoints are often the weakest link in the security chain. They are often used by employees who may not be as security-aware as IT professionals, making them susceptible to social engineering attacks, such as phishing. They may also be running outdated or unpatched software, making them vulnerable to known exploits.

Third, endpoints are often targeted by sophisticated attacks, such as advanced persistent threats (APTs). These attacks are designed to evade traditional security measures and can remain undetected for long periods, allowing attackers to steal data or establish a persistent presence on your network.

One of the most fundamental endpoint security controls is antivirus software. Antivirus software is designed to detect and remove malware, such as viruses, worms, and Trojans. It works by scanning files and processes on an endpoint for known malware signatures. When a match is found, the antivirus software can quarantine or delete the infected file, preventing it from causing harm.

While antivirus software is an essential component of endpoint protection, it is not a silver bullet. Traditional antivirus software relies on signature-based detection, which means it can only detect known malware. It is not effective against new or unknown malware, such as zero-day exploits.

To address this limitation, many antivirus vendors have developed more advanced endpoint protection solutions that use a variety of techniques to detect and prevent malware. These techniques include heuristic analysis, behavior-based detection, and sandboxing.

Heuristic analysis involves examining the code of a file to identify suspicious characteristics that may indicate it is malicious. Behavior-based detection involves monitoring the behavior of programs and processes on an endpoint to identify suspicious activity, such as attempts to access sensitive files or modify system settings. Sandboxing involves running suspicious files in an isolated environment to observe their behavior without risking harm to the endpoint.

Endpoint detection and response (EDR) solutions are another important component of endpoint protection. EDR solutions provide advanced threat detection, investigation, and response capabilities. They continuously monitor endpoints for suspicious activity and provide security teams with the tools they need to investigate and respond to incidents.

EDR solutions work by collecting detailed telemetry data from endpoints, such as process execution, network connections, and file modifications. This data is then analyzed using various techniques, such as machine learning and behavioral analytics, to identify potential threats.

When a potential threat is detected, EDR solutions can generate alerts and provide security teams with detailed information about the incident. This information can include the affected endpoint, the type of threat, the process or file involved, and the actions taken by the threat.

EDR solutions also provide response capabilities, allowing security teams to take action to contain and remediate threats. This can include isolating the affected endpoint from the network, terminating malicious processes, and deleting infected files.

Another important aspect of endpoint protection is patch management. Patch management is the process of keeping software up-to-date with the latest security patches. Software vendors regularly release patches to fix vulnerabilities that could be exploited by cybercriminals.

Failing to install these patches can leave your endpoints vulnerable to attack. Many high-profile data breaches have been caused by attackers exploiting known vulnerabilities in unpatched software.

Patch management can be a challenging task, especially in large organizations with many different types of endpoints and software applications. It requires a systematic approach to identify, test, and deploy patches in a timely manner.

Automated patch management tools can help to streamline this process. These tools can automatically scan endpoints for missing patches, download the patches from vendor websites, and deploy them to the appropriate endpoints.

Application whitelisting is another important endpoint security control. Application whitelisting allows you to specify which applications are allowed to run on your endpoints. Any application that is not on the whitelist is blocked from running.

Application whitelisting can be an effective way to prevent malware from running on your endpoints. However, it can also be challenging to implement and manage, especially in dynamic environments where new applications are frequently installed.

Another approach to application control is application blacklisting. Application blacklisting allows you to specify which applications are not allowed to run on your endpoints. Any application that is on the blacklist is blocked from running.

Application blacklisting is generally easier to implement than application whitelisting, but it is less effective. It relies on knowing which applications are malicious, which can be difficult in the constantly evolving threat landscape.

Full disk encryption (FDE) is another important endpoint security control. FDE encrypts the entire hard drive of an endpoint, making the data unreadable to anyone who does not have the correct encryption key.

FDE is particularly important for laptops and other mobile devices that are at risk of being lost or stolen. If a laptop with FDE is lost or stolen, the data on the hard drive will be protected, even if the attacker removes the hard drive and tries to access it on another computer.

Most modern operating systems include built-in support for FDE. For example, Windows has BitLocker, and macOS has FileVault. There are also third-party FDE solutions available.

Data loss prevention (DLP) is another important aspect of endpoint protection. DLP solutions are designed to prevent sensitive data from leaving your organization without authorization. They work by monitoring data in use, data in motion, and data at rest for sensitive information, such as credit card numbers, social security numbers, and other personally identifiable information (PII).

When a DLP solution detects sensitive data being transmitted or stored in an unauthorized manner, it can take action to prevent the data from leaving your organization. This can include blocking the transmission, encrypting the data, or generating an alert.

DLP solutions can be implemented at the network level, the endpoint level, or both. Endpoint DLP solutions monitor data on individual endpoints, while network DLP solutions monitor data as it travels across the network.

Mobile device management (MDM) is another important aspect of endpoint protection, particularly in organizations that allow employees to use their own devices for work purposes (BYOD). MDM solutions allow you to manage and secure mobile devices that connect to your network.

MDM solutions typically provide features such as device enrollment, configuration management, application management, and security policy enforcement. They allow you to remotely configure devices, install and update applications, and enforce security policies, such as password requirements and encryption settings.

MDM solutions can also be used to remotely wipe or lock devices that are lost or stolen, preventing unauthorized access to sensitive data. They can also be used to track the location of devices, which can be helpful in recovering lost or stolen devices.

In addition to these technical controls, it's also important to have strong security policies and procedures in place for endpoints. These policies should define how endpoints should be used, who is allowed to access them, and what security measures should be in place.

Your endpoint security policies should cover topics such as password management, software installation, data handling, and incident reporting. They should be regularly reviewed and updated to ensure that they remain relevant and effective.

It's also important to provide regular security awareness training to your employees on endpoint security. Your employees are often the first line of defense against cyber attacks, and they need to be aware of the threats they face and how to protect themselves and your organization.

Security awareness training should cover topics such as phishing, malware, social engineering, and password security. It should be tailored to your specific industry and the types of threats that your employees are most likely to encounter.

Endpoint protection is a critical component of any cybersecurity program. By implementing the appropriate controls, monitoring your endpoints for suspicious activity, and providing regular security awareness training to your employees, you can significantly reduce your risk of a cyber attack and protect your valuable data and systems.

The specific endpoint protection measures that you need to implement will depend on your organization's unique needs and circumstances. Factors to consider include the types of endpoints you have, the sensitivity of the data they handle, the industry you operate in, and the regulatory requirements you need to comply with.

It's important to take a layered approach to endpoint protection, implementing multiple controls that work together to provide comprehensive protection. This can include antivirus software,

EDR solutions, patch management, application whitelisting, full disk encryption, DLP, and MDM.

It's also important to regularly review and update your endpoint protection measures to ensure that they remain effective against the latest threats. The cybersecurity landscape is constantly evolving, and new threats and vulnerabilities are emerging all the time.

You should regularly assess your endpoint security posture, identify any weaknesses or gaps, and make necessary improvements. This may involve conducting vulnerability scans, penetration tests, and security audits.

You should also stay informed about the latest threats and vulnerabilities and adapt your endpoint protection measures accordingly. This may involve subscribing to security newsletters and blogs, attending security conferences and workshops, and engaging with external security experts.

In addition to protecting your endpoints from external threats, it's also important to consider the insider threat. Insider threats are security risks that originate from within your organization. They can be malicious insiders who intentionally seek to harm your organization, or they can be negligent employees who unintentionally compromise security through their actions.

To mitigate the insider threat, it's important to implement strong access controls and least privilege principles. This means that users should only have access to the data and systems that they need to perform their jobs. This helps to limit the potential damage that can be caused by a compromised account.

It's also important to monitor user activity for suspicious behavior. This can involve using security information and event management (SIEM) systems to collect and analyze logs from various sources, including endpoints.

User and entity behavior analytics (UEBA) is a relatively new technology that can help to detect insider threats. UEBA solutions use machine learning algorithms to analyze user behavior and identify anomalies that may indicate a security incident.

For example, a UEBA solution might detect that a user is accessing an unusually large number of files or is accessing files at unusual times. This could indicate that the user is attempting to steal data or that their account has been compromised.

Endpoint protection is not just about implementing technical controls; it's also about creating a culture of security awareness within your organization. This involves fostering a shared sense of responsibility for security and encouraging employees to report any suspicious activity or potential security incidents.

By creating a culture of security awareness, you can empower your employees to be your first line of defense against cyber threats. They can help to identify and report potential security incidents, preventing them from escalating into major breaches.

Endpoint protection is a complex and ongoing process that requires a combination of technical controls, policies, procedures, and user awareness. By taking a comprehensive and proactive approach to endpoint protection, you can significantly reduce your risk of a cyber attack and protect your valuable data and systems. As a manager, your role in this is to ensure that endpoint security is prioritized, that the necessary resources are allocated, and that a culture of security awareness is fostered throughout the organization. This commitment to securing the endpoints is not just an IT responsibility; it's a business imperative that safeguards your operations, your reputation, and your future in the digital age.

CHAPTER TEN: Cloud Security Considerations

In our exploration of the multifaceted world of cybersecurity, we've covered the essentials: understanding the threat landscape, identifying digital assets, assessing risks, building a strategy, implementing security frameworks, navigating data protection regulations, fortifying network security, and securing endpoints. Now, we venture into a domain that has revolutionized the way businesses operate and store data—the cloud.

Cloud computing has become ubiquitous, offering unparalleled scalability, flexibility, and cost-effectiveness. It allows businesses to access computing resources—such as servers, storage, databases, networking, software, analytics, and intelligence—over the Internet ("the cloud") instead of owning and maintaining their own physical infrastructure. This shift to the cloud has brought immense benefits, but it has also introduced a new set of security challenges that managers need to understand.

At its core, cloud computing is the delivery of different types of computing services over the internet. These services are typically provided by third-party providers, known as cloud service providers (CSPs), and are offered under various service models, such as Infrastructure as a Service (IaaS), Platform as a Service (PaaS), and Software as a Service (SaaS).

In the IaaS model, the CSP provides virtualized computing resources, such as virtual machines, storage, and networks, over the internet. The customer is responsible for managing the operating systems, applications, and data running on these resources. This model offers the most flexibility and control to the customer but also requires the most technical expertise to manage.

In the PaaS model, the CSP provides a platform that allows customers to develop, run, and manage applications without the complexity of building and maintaining the underlying infrastructure. The CSP manages the infrastructure, including the operating systems, servers, storage, and networks, while the customer manages the applications and data. This model offers less control than IaaS but is more convenient for developers.

In the SaaS model, the CSP provides access to software applications over the internet, typically on a subscription basis. The CSP manages the entire infrastructure, including the applications, data, operating systems, servers, and networks. The customer simply uses the software through a web browser or a mobile app. This model offers the least control but is the easiest to use.

While cloud computing offers numerous advantages, it also introduces unique security considerations. One of the primary concerns is the shared responsibility model. In a traditional on-premises environment, the organization is responsible for the security of its entire infrastructure. However, in a cloud environment, the responsibility for security is shared between the CSP and the customer.

The shared responsibility model varies depending on the cloud service model. In an IaaS environment, the CSP is responsible for the security of the underlying infrastructure, such as the physical security of the data centers, the network infrastructure, and the virtualization layer. The customer is responsible for the security of the operating systems, applications, and data running on the virtual machines.

In a PaaS environment, the CSP is responsible for the security of the platform, including the operating systems, servers, storage, and networks. The customer is responsible for the security of the applications and data running on the platform.

In a SaaS environment, the CSP is responsible for the security of the entire infrastructure, including the applications, data, operating systems, servers, and networks. The customer is typically responsible for managing user access and ensuring that users follow security best practices.

Understanding the shared responsibility model is crucial for ensuring the security of your cloud environment. You need to know which aspects of security are your responsibility and which are the responsibility of your CSP. This information is typically outlined in the service level agreement (SLA) that you sign with your CSP.

Another important security consideration in the cloud is data security. When you store data in the cloud, you are essentially entrusting it to a third party. You need to ensure that your data is adequately protected, both in transit and at rest.

Data in transit refers to data that is being transmitted over a network, such as the internet. Data at rest refers to data that is stored on a storage device, such as a hard drive or a solid-state drive.

To protect data in transit, you should use encryption. Encryption scrambles data so that it is unreadable to anyone who does not have the correct decryption key. Most CSPs offer encryption for data in transit, typically using protocols such as Transport Layer Security (TLS) or Secure Sockets Layer (SSL).

To protect data at rest, you should also use encryption. Many CSPs offer encryption for data at rest, either at the disk level or at the file level. Disk-level encryption encrypts the entire storage volume, while file-level encryption encrypts individual files.

In addition to encryption, you should also implement strong access controls to protect your data in the cloud. Access controls determine who can access your data and what they can do with it. You should use strong passwords, multi-factor authentication, and the principle of least privilege to control access to your data.

Another important security consideration in the cloud is identity and access management (IAM). IAM is the process of managing user identities and controlling their access to resources. In a cloud environment, IAM is crucial for ensuring that only authorized users can access your resources and that they can only access the resources they need to perform their jobs.

Most CSPs offer IAM services that allow you to manage user identities, create roles and groups, and define access policies. You should use these services to create a robust IAM framework that aligns with your organization's security policies.

You should also regularly audit your IAM settings to ensure that they are still appropriate and that there are no unauthorized users or excessive privileges. You should also monitor user activity for any suspicious behavior.

Network security is also important in the cloud, even though you do not have direct control over the physical network infrastructure. You should use the network security features offered by your CSP to create a secure network environment for your resources.

For example, most CSPs offer virtual private clouds (VPCs), which allow you to create a logically isolated section of the cloud network where you can launch your resources. You can define your own IP address range, create subnets, and configure route tables and network gateways.

You can also use security groups and network access control lists (ACLs) to control traffic to and from your resources. Security groups act as virtual firewalls for your instances, controlling inbound and outbound traffic at the instance level. Network ACLs act as firewalls at the subnet level, controlling inbound and outbound traffic for your subnets.

Another important security consideration in the cloud is compliance. Depending on your industry and the type of data you handle, you may need to comply with various regulations, such as the General Data Protection Regulation (GDPR), the Health Insurance Portability and Accountability Act (HIPAA), or the Payment Card Industry Data Security Standard (PCI DSS).

Most CSPs offer features and services to help you meet your compliance obligations. For example, they may offer encryption, access controls, audit logs, and other security features that are required by various regulations.

However, it's important to remember that using a compliant CSP does not automatically make you compliant. You still need to configure and use the CSP's services in a compliant manner. You also need to ensure that your own applications and processes are compliant with the relevant regulations.

You should also regularly assess your cloud environment for compliance and make any necessary changes to ensure that you remain compliant. This may involve conducting regular audits, vulnerability scans, and penetration tests.

Another important security consideration in the cloud is incident response. Despite your best efforts, security incidents can still occur in the cloud. You need to have a plan in place for responding to these incidents quickly and effectively.

Your incident response plan should include procedures for detecting, analyzing, containing, eradicating, and recovering from security incidents. It should also include clear roles and responsibilities, communication protocols, and escalation procedures.

You should regularly test your incident response plan to ensure that it is effective and that everyone knows what to do in the event of an incident. This can be done through tabletop exercises, simulations, or even live-fire drills.

You should also work closely with your CSP to coordinate your incident response efforts. Most CSPs offer incident response services and support to help you respond to security incidents.

In addition to these technical considerations, it's also important to have strong security policies and procedures in place for your cloud environment. These policies should define how your cloud resources should be used, who is allowed to access them, and what security measures should be in place.

Your cloud security policies should cover topics such as access management, data protection, network security, incident response, and compliance. They should be regularly reviewed and updated to ensure that they remain relevant and effective.

It's also important to provide regular security awareness training to your employees on cloud security. Your employees need to be aware of the unique security challenges of the cloud and how to protect themselves and your organization.

Security awareness training should cover topics such as the shared responsibility model, data security, access controls, and incident reporting. It should be tailored to your specific cloud environment and the types of threats that your employees are most likely to encounter.

Cloud security is a complex and constantly evolving field. New threats and vulnerabilities are emerging all the time, and you need to stay up-to-date on the latest security best practices.

One way to stay informed is to subscribe to security newsletters and blogs that focus on cloud security. These resources can provide you with valuable information about the latest threats, vulnerabilities, and security technologies.

You can also attend cloud security conferences and workshops. These events provide an opportunity to learn from security experts and network with other professionals in the field.

Another important resource is your CSP. Your CSP can provide you with valuable information about their security features and how to use them effectively. They can also provide you with support in the event of a security incident.

Cloud computing offers numerous benefits for businesses, but it also introduces unique security challenges. By understanding the shared responsibility model, implementing strong data security and access controls, configuring network security features, ensuring compliance, having an incident response plan, and providing regular security awareness training, you can significantly reduce your risk of a cyber attack in the cloud and protect your valuable data and systems. As a manager, your role in this is to ensure that cloud security is prioritized, that the necessary resources are allocated, and that a culture of security awareness is fostered throughout the organization. This proactive approach to cloud security is not just an IT responsibility; it's a business imperative that safeguards your operations, your reputation, and your future in the digital age.

CHAPTER ELEVEN: Identity and Access Management

Having navigated the foundational aspects of cybersecurity, including securing networks and endpoints, and understanding the nuances of cloud security, we now arrive at a critical juncture: managing who has access to what within your organization. This is the realm of Identity and Access Management (IAM), a cornerstone of any robust cybersecurity program. It's about ensuring that the right people have the right access to the right resources at the right time, and for the right reasons.

In today's interconnected world, where employees, contractors, partners, and customers often require access to various digital assets, managing identities and access has become increasingly complex. A well-designed IAM framework not only enhances security but also improves operational efficiency, streamlines user experience, and ensures compliance with various regulations.

At its core, IAM is about managing digital identities and controlling their access to your organization's resources. A digital identity is a collection of attributes that uniquely identifies a user, device, or application within your digital ecosystem. These attributes can include usernames, passwords, email addresses, roles, permissions, and other relevant information.

The primary goal of IAM is to ensure that only authorized individuals can access specific resources based on their roles and responsibilities. This is achieved through a combination of processes, policies, and technologies that work together to manage the entire lifecycle of a digital identity, from creation and provisioning to modification and eventual deactivation.

One of the fundamental components of IAM is authentication. Authentication is the process of verifying the identity of a user, device, or application attempting to access a resource. It's about proving that someone is who they claim to be. There are several methods of authentication, commonly categorized as something you know, something you have, and something you are.

Something you know typically refers to a password or a PIN. This is the most common form of authentication, but it's also the weakest. Passwords can be guessed, stolen, or cracked, especially if they are weak or reused across multiple accounts.

Something you have typically refers to a physical token, such as a smart card, a security token, or a mobile device. This form of authentication adds an extra layer of security by requiring the user to possess a physical object in addition to knowing a password.

Something you are refers to biometric authentication, such as fingerprint scanning, facial recognition, or voice recognition. This form of authentication is based on unique biological characteristics and is generally considered to be more secure than passwords or tokens.

Multi-factor authentication (MFA) combines two or more of these authentication methods to provide a higher level of security. For example, you might be required to enter a password (something you know) and then enter a code sent to your mobile phone (something you have). MFA significantly reduces the risk of unauthorized access, even if one factor is compromised.

Another important component of IAM is authorization. Authorization is the process of determining what resources an authenticated user is allowed to access and what actions they are permitted to perform. It's about granting the appropriate level of access based on the user's role and responsibilities.

Authorization is typically based on access control policies that define which users or groups have access to which resources. These policies can be implemented using various access control models, such as role-based access control (RBAC), attribute-based access control (ABAC), or discretionary access control (DAC).

Role-based access control (RBAC) is the most common access control model. In RBAC, access permissions are assigned to roles rather than individual users. Users are then assigned to one or more roles based on their job functions. This simplifies access management, especially in large organizations with many users and roles.

For example, you might have a "sales" role that has access to the CRM system and a "finance" role that has access to the accounting system. Users in the sales department would be assigned to the "sales" role, and users in the finance department would be assigned to the "finance" role.

Attribute-based access control (ABAC) is a more granular access control model that allows you to define access policies based on attributes of the user, the resource, and the environment. For example, you might have a policy that allows users in the "sales" role to access the CRM system only during business hours and only from a corporate-owned device.

Discretionary access control (DAC) is a less common access control model that allows resource owners to determine who has access to their resources. This model is often used in operating systems to control access to files and directories.

Another important aspect of IAM is identity governance. Identity governance is the process of managing and monitoring user access to ensure that it remains appropriate and compliant with your organization's policies and regulations. It's about maintaining oversight and control over who has access to what.

Identity governance involves several key activities, such as access certification, access request management, and privileged access management.

Access certification is the process of periodically reviewing user access to ensure that it is still appropriate. This involves having managers or other designated individuals review the access rights of their subordinates and confirm that they are still needed. Any access that is no longer required should be revoked.

Access request management is the process of handling requests for new or changed access. This involves establishing a formal process for users to request access to resources, for managers to approve or deny those requests, and for IT staff to provision the access.

Privileged access management (PAM) is the process of managing and monitoring access to your organization's most sensitive resources. Privileged accounts, such as administrator accounts, have elevated privileges that allow them to perform actions that can have a significant impact on your systems and data.

PAM solutions help to secure these privileged accounts by providing features such as password vaulting, session monitoring, and just-in-time access. Password vaulting stores privileged account passwords in a secure vault and automatically rotates them on a regular basis. Session monitoring allows you to monitor and record the activities of privileged users in real time. Just-in-time access grants privileged access only when it is needed and for a limited period.

Another important aspect of IAM is single sign-on (SSO). SSO allows users to authenticate once and then access multiple applications and resources without having to re-authenticate each time. This improves the user experience and reduces the number of passwords that users need to remember.

SSO works by establishing a trust relationship between the applications and a central identity provider. When a user authenticates to the identity provider, they are issued a token that they can then use to access the other applications.

SSO can also enhance security by reducing the risk of password reuse and by allowing you to enforce stronger authentication policies, such as multi-factor authentication, for all your applications.

Implementing an IAM solution can be a complex undertaking, especially in large organizations with many users, applications, and systems. It requires careful planning, coordination, and execution.

The first step in implementing an IAM solution is to define your requirements. This involves identifying your users, the resources they need to access, and the policies that govern their access. You should also consider your organization's security and compliance requirements.

Next, you need to choose an IAM solution that meets your requirements. There are many IAM solutions available, ranging from simple cloud-based services to complex on-premises systems. You should evaluate the features, scalability, and cost of each solution to determine which one is the best fit for your organization.

Once you have chosen an IAM solution, you need to integrate it with your existing systems and applications. This may involve configuring your applications to use the IAM solution for authentication and authorization, or it may involve developing custom integrations.

After integrating your systems and applications, you need to provision user identities and assign them the appropriate access rights. This may involve importing user data from existing directories, such as Active Directory, or creating new user accounts.

Once your IAM solution is up and running, you need to monitor it regularly to ensure that it is functioning properly and that your security policies are being enforced. You should also regularly review and update your IAM policies and procedures to ensure that they remain relevant and effective.

Implementing an IAM framework is not just about deploying technology; it's also about establishing processes and policies that govern how identities and access are managed within your organization. These processes and policies should be documented and regularly reviewed to ensure that they remain aligned with your business objectives and security requirements.

One of the key processes to establish is a user onboarding process. This process should define how new users are added to your systems, what information needs to be collected, and what approvals are required. It should also specify how user identities are created and provisioned with the appropriate access rights.

Another important process is a user offboarding process. This process should define how user access is revoked when an employee leaves the organization or changes roles. It's crucial to ensure that access is removed promptly to prevent unauthorized access to sensitive data.

You should also establish a process for managing access requests. This process should define how users can request access to resources, how managers can approve or deny those requests, and how IT staff can provision the access.

In addition to these processes, you should also establish policies that govern how identities and access are managed within your organization. These policies should cover topics such as password complexity, account lockout, access certification, and privileged access management.

Your policies should be communicated to all employees and regularly reviewed to ensure that they remain relevant and effective. You should also provide regular training to your employees on these policies and on the importance of identity and access management.

IAM is not just an IT function; it's a business function that requires collaboration between IT, HR, legal, and other departments. IT is typically responsible for implementing and managing the IAM technology, while HR is responsible for managing employee data and ensuring that access is aligned with job roles. Legal may be involved in defining policies and ensuring compliance with regulations.

It's important to establish clear roles and responsibilities for IAM within your organization. This helps to ensure that everyone knows what is expected of them and that there is accountability for managing identities and access.

As a manager, you play a critical role in ensuring the success of your organization's IAM program. You need to understand the importance of IAM and advocate for its implementation and ongoing management. You also need to ensure that your team members are aware of their responsibilities related to IAM and that they follow the established policies and procedures.

You should also work with your IT department to ensure that your team members have the access they need to perform their jobs while also adhering to the principle of least privilege. This means that users should only have access to the resources they absolutely need and nothing more.

Furthermore, you should regularly review the access rights of your team members to ensure that they are still appropriate. If an employee changes roles or leaves the organization, their access should be promptly updated or revoked.

By taking an active role in IAM, you can help to ensure that your organization's digital assets are protected and that your employees have the access they need to be productive.

The benefits of a well-implemented IAM program are numerous. First and foremost, it enhances security by reducing the risk of unauthorized access to sensitive data and systems. By ensuring that only authorized users can access specific resources, you can prevent data breaches, protect intellectual property, and maintain the confidentiality, integrity, and availability of your digital assets.

IAM also improves operational efficiency by automating many of the manual processes associated with managing user access. This can save time and reduce costs for your IT department, allowing them to focus on other strategic initiatives.

Moreover, IAM can improve the user experience by simplifying access to resources. With features like single sign-on, users can access multiple applications with a single set of credentials, eliminating the need to remember multiple passwords and reducing password fatigue.

IAM also plays a crucial role in ensuring compliance with various regulations, such as the GDPR, HIPAA, and SOX. These regulations often require organizations to demonstrate that they have adequate controls in place to protect sensitive data and to provide an audit trail of user activity. A well-designed IAM framework can help you meet these requirements by providing detailed logs of who accessed what and when.

In conclusion, Identity and Access Management is a fundamental component of any robust cybersecurity program. It's about managing digital identities, controlling access to resources, and ensuring that the right people have the right access at the right time. By implementing a comprehensive IAM framework, you can enhance security, improve operational efficiency, streamline user experience, and ensure compliance with regulations. While the implementation of such a system requires careful planning, collaboration, and ongoing management, the benefits far outweigh the challenges. As a manager, your understanding and support of IAM are vital to its success and, consequently, to the overall security and resilience of your organization in the digital age.

CHAPTER TWELVE: Security Awareness Training for Employees

Throughout our exploration of cybersecurity, we've delved into the technical intricacies of securing networks, endpoints, and cloud environments. We've examined the strategic importance of frameworks, the legal obligations of data protection, and the critical role of identity and access management. Now, we arrive at a component of cybersecurity that is often cited as both the strongest and weakest link in an organization's defenses: the human element.

No matter how sophisticated your technical controls are, they can be undermined by a single, unintentional mistake by an employee. A misplaced click on a phishing email, a weak password reused across multiple accounts, or a sensitive document left unprotected can all lead to a security breach. This is why security awareness training is not just an optional add-on; it's a fundamental necessity for any organization that wants to protect its digital assets.

Security awareness training is the process of educating employees about the various cybersecurity threats they may encounter and how to recognize and respond to them. It's about equipping them with the knowledge and skills they need to protect themselves and your organization from cyber attacks. It's not about turning employees into cybersecurity experts, but rather about making them aware of the risks, their responsibilities, and the best practices they should follow to maintain a secure environment.

The goal of security awareness training is to change employee behavior and foster a culture of security awareness within your organization. It's about creating a human firewall, where every employee understands their role in protecting sensitive data and systems. This involves not only providing information but also engaging employees in a way that resonates with them and motivates them to adopt secure practices.

One of the most common topics covered in security awareness training is phishing. Phishing attacks are a type of social engineering where attackers use deceptive emails, messages, or websites to trick individuals into divulging sensitive information, such as usernames, passwords, or credit card details. Phishing attacks are often the first step in a larger cyber attack, and they can be incredibly effective if employees are not trained to recognize them.

Security awareness training should educate employees about the various types of phishing attacks, such as spear phishing, whaling, and vishing, and how to identify them. This includes teaching them to recognize the common red flags of phishing emails, such as:

- **Suspicious sender addresses:** The email address may be misspelled or may not match the organization the email claims to be from.

- **Generic greetings:** The email may use a generic greeting, such as "Dear Customer," instead of the recipient's name.

- **Urgent or threatening language:** The email may create a sense of urgency or use threatening language to pressure the recipient into taking immediate action.

- **Requests for sensitive information:** The email may ask the recipient to provide sensitive information, such as their password or credit card details.

- **Suspicious links or attachments:** The email may contain links to malicious websites or attachments that contain malware.

Training should also emphasize the importance of verifying the authenticity of an email before clicking on any links or opening any attachments. Employees should be encouraged to hover over links to see the actual URL they point to and to be cautious of any links that look suspicious. They should also be advised against opening attachments from unknown or untrusted senders.

Another important topic covered in security awareness training is malware. Malware, short for malicious software, is any software designed to harm or disrupt a computer system or network. Malware can take many forms, including viruses, worms, Trojans, ransomware, and spyware.

Security awareness training should educate employees about the different types of malware and how they can infect their devices. This includes explaining how malware can be spread through email attachments, infected websites, malicious software downloads, and even compromised USB drives.

Training should also emphasize the importance of keeping their devices and software up-to-date with the latest security patches. Software vendors regularly release patches to fix vulnerabilities that could be exploited by malware. Failing to install these patches can leave devices vulnerable to attack.

Employees should also be trained on the importance of using strong, unique passwords for all their accounts. Passwords should be at least 12 characters long and include a mix of uppercase and lowercase letters, numbers, and symbols. They should also be advised against using the same password for multiple accounts.

Password managers can be a valuable tool for helping employees create and manage strong, unique passwords. Password managers are software applications that store passwords in an encrypted format and can automatically generate strong passwords.

Social engineering is another important topic that should be covered in security awareness training. Social engineering is a technique used by attackers to manipulate individuals into divulging sensitive information or performing actions that compromise security. Social engineering attacks can take many forms, including phishing, baiting, pretexting, and tailgating.

Baiting involves offering something enticing to lure a victim into a trap. For example, an attacker might leave a USB drive labeled "Salary Information" in a public area, hoping that someone will pick it up and plug it into their computer. The USB drive might contain malware that infects the computer when it is plugged in.

Pretexting involves creating a false scenario to trick a victim into divulging information or performing an action. For example, an attacker might call an employee pretending to be from the IT department and ask for their password to troubleshoot a problem.

Tailgating involves following someone through a secure entrance without authorization. For example, an attacker might follow an employee through a door that requires a keycard to enter.

Security awareness training should educate employees about these and other social engineering techniques and how to recognize and resist them. This includes teaching them to be wary of unsolicited requests for information, to verify the identity of anyone asking for sensitive information, and to never allow someone to follow them through a secure entrance without proper authorization.

Data handling is another crucial topic for security awareness training. Employees need to understand the importance of protecting sensitive data and how to handle it properly. This includes understanding the different classifications of data, such as confidential, internal, and public, and the appropriate handling procedures for each classification.

Employees should be trained on how to securely store, transmit, and dispose of sensitive data. This includes using encryption to protect data in transit and at rest, using secure file-sharing services, and properly disposing of physical documents containing sensitive information.

They should also be made aware of the potential consequences of mishandling sensitive data, such as data breaches, legal liabilities, and reputational damage.

Incident reporting is another vital component of security awareness training. Employees need to know how to report a potential security incident, such as a suspected phishing email, a lost or stolen device, or any other suspicious activity.

Organizations should have a clear and easy-to-use incident reporting process in place. This may involve a dedicated email address, a phone number, or an online form. Employees should be encouraged to report any potential security incidents, even if they are not sure if it is a real threat.

Prompt reporting of incidents can help to prevent them from escalating into major breaches. It also allows the security team to investigate the incident, take appropriate action, and learn from it to prevent similar incidents in the future.

Security awareness training should not be a one-time event. It should be an ongoing process that is regularly reinforced and updated to reflect the latest threats and best practices. This can involve sending out regular security newsletters, conducting simulated phishing exercises, and providing refresher training on a periodic basis.

Simulated phishing exercises can be a particularly effective way to test employees' ability to recognize and respond to phishing attacks. These exercises involve sending out fake phishing emails to employees and tracking their responses. Those who fall for the simulated attack can then be provided with additional training and guidance.

The frequency and format of security awareness training will depend on your organization's specific needs and circumstances. Factors to consider include the size of your organization, the industry you operate in, the sensitivity of the data you handle, and the regulatory requirements you need to comply with.

It's also important to tailor the training to the specific roles and responsibilities of your employees. For example, employees who handle sensitive data or have access to critical systems may require more in-depth training than those who do not.

The delivery method for security awareness training can also vary. It can be delivered in person, through online courses, or a combination of both. Online courses offer the advantage of being self-paced and can be accessed from anywhere, while in-person training allows for more interaction and engagement.

Regardless of the delivery method, it's important to make the training engaging and interactive. This can involve using real-world examples, incorporating gamification elements, and providing opportunities for employees to ask questions and discuss the material.

Measuring the effectiveness of security awareness training is crucial to ensure that it is having the desired impact. This can involve tracking metrics such as the number of employees who complete the training, the results of simulated phishing exercises, and the number of security incidents reported.

It's also important to gather feedback from employees on the training to identify areas for improvement. This can be done through surveys, focus groups, or informal conversations.

Security awareness training is not just about educating employees; it's also about creating a culture of security awareness within your organization. This involves fostering a shared sense of responsibility for security and encouraging employees to be vigilant and proactive in protecting sensitive data and systems.

Creating a culture of security awareness requires buy-in from all levels of the organization, from the top executives to the front-line employees. It involves communicating the importance of security, recognizing and rewarding good security practices, and providing ongoing support and resources.

As a manager, you play a critical role in fostering a culture of security awareness within your team. You can do this by setting a good example, communicating the importance of security, and providing your team members with the resources and support they need to be secure.

You should also encourage your team members to report any potential security incidents and to ask questions if they are unsure about something. Creating an open and supportive environment where employees feel comfortable discussing security issues is essential for building a strong security culture.

Security awareness training is a vital component of any comprehensive cybersecurity program. By educating employees about the various threats they may encounter and how to recognize and respond to them, you can significantly reduce your organization's risk of a cyber attack.

It's important to remember that security awareness training is not a one-size-fits-all solution. It needs to be tailored to your organization's specific needs and circumstances, taking into account your industry, your size, your technology infrastructure, and your risk tolerance.

It's also important to remember that security awareness training is not a one-time event. It's an ongoing process that requires regular reinforcement and updates to reflect the changing threat landscape.

By investing in security awareness training and fostering a culture of security awareness, you can empower your employees to be your first line of defense against cyber threats. You can transform your workforce from a potential vulnerability into a powerful asset in your fight against cybercrime. This human element, often overlooked in the technical discussions of cybersecurity, is a critical investment in the overall resilience and security posture of your organization. By prioritizing security awareness training, you are not just protecting your data and systems; you are cultivating a security-conscious workforce that is prepared to meet the challenges of the digital age.

CHAPTER THIRTEEN: Incident Response Planning

In our comprehensive journey through the world of cybersecurity, we've explored the threat landscape, identified our digital assets, assessed risks, built a strategy, implemented frameworks, understood data protection regulations, and fortified our networks, endpoints, and cloud environments. We've even empowered our employees through security awareness training. Yet, despite all these proactive measures, there remains an undeniable truth: security incidents can and do happen. No organization is entirely immune to cyber threats, regardless of how well-prepared they may be.

This is where incident response planning comes into play. It's about acknowledging that despite our best efforts, breaches can occur, and being prepared to respond effectively when they do. An incident response plan is a documented, systematic approach to handling security incidents, minimizing their impact, and ensuring a swift and effective recovery. It's the playbook that guides your organization through the chaos of a security incident, providing a clear set of procedures, roles, and responsibilities.

Think of an incident response plan as a fire drill for your digital infrastructure. Just as a fire drill prepares building occupants to respond calmly and effectively in the event of a fire, an incident response plan prepares your organization to respond to a security incident in a coordinated and efficient manner. Without a plan, you're left scrambling in the dark, wasting valuable time and potentially exacerbating the damage.

The primary goal of incident response planning is to minimize the impact of a security incident and to restore normal operations as quickly as possible. This involves detecting and analyzing the incident, containing it to prevent further damage, eradicating the threat, recovering affected systems and data, and learning from the incident to improve future responses.

Building an effective incident response plan is not solely an IT function. It requires collaboration and input from across the organization, including legal, human resources, communications, and senior management. This ensures that the plan aligns with your overall business objectives and that it addresses the specific needs and concerns of each department.

The first step in developing an incident response plan is to establish an incident response team. This team is responsible for coordinating and executing the response to security incidents. The team should be composed of individuals with the necessary skills and expertise to handle various aspects of an incident, such as technical analysis, communication, legal compliance, and decision-making.

The incident response team should include representatives from IT, security, legal, human resources, and public relations. Depending on the nature of your business, you may also want to include representatives from other departments, such as operations, finance, or customer service.

The team leader should be a senior individual with the authority to make decisions and allocate resources. This is often the Chief Information Security Officer (CISO) or a similar role. The team leader is responsible for overseeing the entire incident response process, from detection to recovery.

Each team member should have clearly defined roles and responsibilities. For example, the IT and security representatives might be responsible for technical analysis, containment, and eradication. The legal representative might be responsible for ensuring compliance with relevant regulations and managing any legal issues that arise. The human resources representative might be responsible for handling any internal investigations or disciplinary actions. The public relations representative might be responsible for managing external communications and protecting the organization's reputation.

Once the incident response team is established, the next step is to define what constitutes a security incident. Not every security event is an incident. An incident is typically defined as an event that has the potential to cause harm to your organization's information systems or data, or that violates your security policies.

Examples of security incidents include:

- Unauthorized access to sensitive data

- Malware infections

- Denial-of-service attacks

- Website defacement

- Loss or theft of devices containing sensitive data

- Insider threats

It's important to have a clear definition of what constitutes an incident so that employees know when to report a potential security event to the incident response team. This definition should be communicated to all employees as part of your security awareness training program.

The next step in developing an incident response plan is to define the phases of the incident response process. A common framework for incident response includes the following six phases: preparation, identification, containment, eradication, recovery, and lessons learned.

The preparation phase involves establishing the incident response team, defining roles and responsibilities, developing the incident response plan, and training the team on the plan. It also involves implementing the necessary technical controls and tools to support incident response, such as intrusion detection systems, security information and event management (SIEM) systems, and incident management platforms.

The identification phase involves detecting and analyzing potential security incidents. This can be done through various means, such as monitoring security logs, analyzing alerts from security tools, and receiving reports from employees. When a potential incident is detected, the incident response team must quickly assess the situation to determine whether it is a true incident and, if so, its severity.

The containment phase involves taking steps to limit the damage caused by the incident and prevent it from spreading further. This may involve isolating affected systems from the network, disabling compromised accounts, or blocking malicious traffic. The goal of containment is to stabilize the situation and prevent further harm while the investigation and recovery efforts are underway.

The eradication phase involves removing the threat from the affected systems. This may involve removing malware, patching vulnerabilities, or rebuilding compromised systems. The goal of eradication is to eliminate the root cause of the incident and ensure that the threat is completely removed.

The recovery phase involves restoring affected systems and data to their normal operational state. This may involve restoring data from backups, reinstalling applications, and reconfiguring systems. The goal of recovery is to get the business back up and running as quickly as possible while ensuring that the systems are secure and free from any residual threats.

The lessons learned phase involves conducting a post-incident review to analyze what happened, how well the incident response plan worked, and what improvements can be made. This is a critical phase that is often overlooked, but it is essential for improving your organization's security posture and preventing similar incidents from occurring in the future.

Once you have defined the phases of the incident response process, you need to develop detailed procedures for each phase. These procedures should provide step-by-step instructions on what actions to take, who is responsible for each action, and what tools or resources are needed.

For example, the procedures for the identification phase might include instructions on how to analyze security logs, how to use your SIEM system to investigate alerts, and how to escalate potential incidents to the incident response team.

The procedures for the containment phase might include instructions on how to isolate affected systems from the network, how to disable compromised accounts, and how to block malicious traffic using your firewall or intrusion prevention system.

The procedures for the eradication phase might include instructions on how to remove malware using your antivirus or endpoint detection and response (EDR) solution, how to patch vulnerabilities using your patch management system, and how to rebuild compromised systems from clean backups.

The procedures for the recovery phase might include instructions on how to restore data from backups, how to reinstall applications, and how to reconfigure systems to their original settings.

The procedures for the lessons learned phase might include instructions on how to conduct a post-incident review meeting, how to document the findings of the review, and how to implement any recommended improvements.

In addition to these procedures, your incident response plan should also include communication protocols. These protocols define who needs to be informed about an incident, when they should be informed, and how they should be informed.

The communication protocols should include both internal and external communication procedures. Internal communication involves keeping stakeholders within your organization informed about the incident, such as senior management, legal, human resources, and other relevant departments. External communication involves communicating with external parties, such as customers, partners, regulators, and law enforcement, as needed.

Your communication protocols should also define the roles and responsibilities for communication. For example, the incident response team leader might be responsible for communicating with senior management, while the public relations representative might be responsible for communicating with the media.

It's important to have a clear and consistent communication strategy during an incident. This helps to ensure that everyone is on the same page, that accurate information is being disseminated, and that your organization's reputation is protected.

Another important aspect of incident response planning is to establish relationships with external parties, such as law enforcement, regulators, and cybersecurity experts. These relationships can be invaluable during an incident, providing you with access to resources, expertise, and support that you may not have in-house.

For example, you might want to establish a relationship with a local law enforcement agency that specializes in cybercrime. This can be helpful if you need to report an incident to law enforcement or if you need assistance with an investigation.

You might also want to establish a relationship with a cybersecurity firm that provides incident response services. These firms can provide you with access to specialized expertise and tools that can help you to contain, eradicate, and recover from an incident.

It's also important to understand your legal and regulatory obligations related to incident response. Depending on your industry and the type of data you handle, you may be required to report certain types of incidents to regulators or to notify affected individuals.

For example, if you are subject to the General Data Protection Regulation (GDPR), you are required to report certain types of data breaches to the relevant supervisory authority within 72 hours of becoming aware of the breach. You may also be required to notify the affected individuals without undue delay.

Your incident response plan should include procedures for complying with these legal and regulatory obligations. This may involve working with your legal team to determine your reporting obligations and developing procedures for notifying regulators and affected individuals.

Once your incident response plan is developed, it's crucial to test it regularly. Testing your plan helps to ensure that it is effective, that everyone knows their roles and responsibilities, and that any gaps or weaknesses are identified and addressed.

There are several ways to test your incident response plan, such as tabletop exercises, simulations, and live-fire drills. Tabletop exercises involve bringing the incident response team together to discuss a hypothetical incident scenario and walk through the steps of the plan. Simulations involve using simulated attacks to test your technical controls and your team's ability to detect and respond to them. Live-fire drills involve conducting a full-scale simulation of an incident, including all phases of the response process.

Regular testing helps to keep the incident response team prepared and ensures that the plan remains relevant and effective. It also provides an opportunity to identify areas for improvement and to update the plan accordingly.

In addition to testing the plan itself, it's also important to provide regular training to the incident response team and to all employees on their roles and responsibilities during an incident. This training should cover the incident response process, the communication protocols, and any relevant technical tools or procedures.

Training should be tailored to the specific roles and responsibilities of each individual. For example, the incident response team members may require more in-depth technical training on how to use incident response tools and how to conduct forensic analysis. All employees should receive training on how to recognize and report potential security incidents.

Incident response planning is an ongoing process that requires regular review and updates. The threat landscape is constantly evolving, and your organization's systems and processes are constantly changing. Therefore, it's essential to regularly review your incident response plan to ensure that it remains relevant and effective.

You should review your plan at least annually, or more frequently if there are significant changes to your organization's systems, processes, or regulatory environment. You should also review your plan after any major security incident to incorporate any lessons learned.

As a manager, you play a critical role in ensuring that your organization has an effective incident response plan in place. You need to understand the importance of incident response planning and advocate for its implementation and ongoing maintenance.

You should also ensure that your team members are aware of their roles and responsibilities during an incident and that they receive the necessary training. You should also work with your IT and security teams to ensure that the necessary technical controls and tools are in place to support incident response.

By taking an active role in incident response planning, you can help to ensure that your organization is prepared to respond effectively to security incidents, minimize their impact, and recover quickly. This proactive approach to incident response is not just an IT responsibility; it's a business imperative that safeguards your operations, your reputation, and your future in the digital age. It demonstrates a commitment to resilience and preparedness, showing stakeholders that you are ready to face the inevitable challenges that come with operating in an interconnected world. By prioritizing incident response planning, you are not just protecting your data and systems; you are cultivating a culture of preparedness that permeates every level of the organization, from the boardroom to the front lines.

CHAPTER FOURTEEN: Disaster Recovery and Business Continuity

In the realm of cybersecurity, we've traversed through understanding the landscape, fortifying our defenses, and planning for incident response. Now, we arrive at a critical juncture that deals with the aftermath of a major disruption: disaster recovery and business continuity. While incident response focuses on addressing specific security incidents, disaster recovery and business continuity planning take a broader view, encompassing the processes, policies, and procedures that ensure your organization can continue to operate or quickly resume operations in the face of a significant disruption, whether it be a cyberattack, a natural disaster, a hardware failure, or any other event that severely impacts your ability to conduct business.

Think of disaster recovery and business continuity as the safety net that ensures your organization's survival and resilience in the face of adversity. It's about having a plan in place to recover from major disruptions and keep your business running, even when faced with the unexpected. It's not just about recovering data and systems; it's about ensuring the continuity of your critical business operations, maintaining your reputation, and minimizing the financial and operational impact of a disaster.

Disaster recovery and business continuity planning are often used interchangeably, but they are distinct, albeit closely related, concepts. Disaster recovery focuses primarily on the IT infrastructure and operations. It's about restoring IT systems, applications, and data after a disruption. Business continuity, on the other hand, takes a broader approach, encompassing the entire organization. It's about ensuring that all critical business functions can continue to operate during and after a disaster.

The primary goal of disaster recovery and business continuity planning is to minimize downtime and data loss. Downtime refers to the period when your systems or services are unavailable, while data loss refers to the permanent loss of data. Both downtime and data loss can have severe consequences for your business, including financial losses, reputational damage, legal liabilities, and loss of customer trust.

The first step in developing a disaster recovery and business continuity plan is to conduct a business impact analysis (BIA). A BIA is a systematic process for identifying and evaluating the potential effects of a disruption to critical business operations. It helps you understand how different types of disasters could impact your business, which functions are most critical, and how quickly you need to recover them.

To conduct a BIA, you need to involve representatives from all key departments within your organization. This ensures that you have a comprehensive understanding of your business operations and that you don't overlook any critical functions. You should identify all your business functions, determine their criticality, and assess the potential impact of a disruption to each function.

The criticality of a business function is typically determined based on factors such as its impact on revenue, its impact on customer service, its regulatory requirements, and its dependencies on other functions. For example, a function that directly generates revenue, such as order processing, is typically considered more critical than a function that does not, such as internal training.

The potential impact of a disruption can be assessed in terms of financial losses, operational disruptions, reputational damage, and legal or regulatory penalties. For example, a disruption to your order processing system could result in lost sales, while a disruption to your customer service system could damage your reputation.

Once you have identified your critical business functions and assessed the potential impact of a disruption, the next step is to determine your recovery time objective (RTO) and recovery point objective (RPO) for each function.

The RTO is the maximum amount of time that a business function can be down without causing unacceptable consequences. For example, if your order processing system can be down for a maximum of four hours without causing significant financial losses, then your RTO for that function is four hours.

The RPO is the maximum amount of data that can be lost without causing unacceptable consequences. For example, if your business can tolerate losing up to one hour's worth of data from your order processing system, then your RPO for that system is one hour.

RTOs and RPOs should be determined based on your business needs and risk tolerance. They should be realistic and achievable, taking into account your available resources and the capabilities of your IT infrastructure.

Once you have determined your RTOs and RPOs, the next step is to develop a disaster recovery plan. This plan outlines the specific procedures and resources needed to recover your IT systems, applications, and data in the event of a disaster.

Your disaster recovery plan should include detailed procedures for restoring your IT infrastructure, such as servers, networks, and storage systems. It should also include procedures for recovering your critical applications and data. These procedures should be documented step-by-step, with clear instructions on what actions to take, who is responsible for each action, and what tools or resources are needed.

Your disaster recovery plan should also identify the resources needed to support the recovery effort. This includes IT personnel, hardware, software, and facilities. You may need to establish relationships with third-party vendors to provide backup hardware, software, or facilities in the event of a disaster.

Another important aspect of disaster recovery planning is data backup and recovery. You need to have a robust data backup strategy in place to ensure that you can recover your critical data in the event of a disaster. This involves regularly backing up your data to a secure location, such as a remote data center or a cloud-based backup service.

Your data backup strategy should be based on your RPO. If your RPO is one hour, then you need to back up your data at least every hour. You should also test your backups regularly to ensure that they are working properly and that you can restore your data from them.

In addition to your disaster recovery plan, you also need to develop a business continuity plan. This plan outlines the procedures and resources needed to keep your critical business functions running during and after a disaster.

Your business continuity plan should address all aspects of your business operations, not just IT. This includes your people, processes, facilities, and supply chain. You need to identify alternative ways to perform your critical business functions if your primary systems or facilities are unavailable.

For example, if your primary office location is inaccessible due to a natural disaster, you may need to have a plan in place to allow your employees to work remotely. This may involve providing them with laptops, VPN access, and other necessary tools.

Your business continuity plan should also include procedures for communicating with your employees, customers, partners, and other stakeholders during a disaster. This is crucial for maintaining trust and confidence in your business during a difficult time.

Once your disaster recovery and business continuity plans are developed, it's essential to test them regularly. Testing helps to ensure that your plans are effective, that your staff knows what to do in the event of a disaster, and that any gaps or weaknesses are identified and addressed.

There are several ways to test your plans, such as tabletop exercises, simulations, and full-scale drills. Tabletop exercises involve bringing together key personnel to discuss a hypothetical disaster scenario and walk through the steps of the plans.

Simulations involve using simulated disruptions to test your technical recovery capabilities. Full-scale drills involve conducting a mock disaster to test your entire response, including both IT recovery and business continuity.

Regular testing helps to keep your plans up-to-date and ensures that your staff is prepared to respond effectively to a real disaster. It also provides an opportunity to identify areas for improvement and to update the plans accordingly.

In addition to testing, it's also important to provide regular training to your employees on their roles and responsibilities in the event of a disaster. This training should cover the disaster recovery and business continuity plans, as well as any relevant technical procedures or tools.

Training should be tailored to the specific roles and responsibilities of each individual. For example, IT staff may require more in-depth technical training on how to restore systems and data, while other employees may only need to be familiar with the overall business continuity plan and their specific role in it.

Disaster recovery and business continuity planning are ongoing processes that require regular review and updates. The threat landscape is constantly evolving, and your business operations are constantly changing. Therefore, it's essential to regularly review your plans to ensure that they remain relevant and effective.

You should review your plans at least annually, or more frequently if there are significant changes to your business operations, IT infrastructure, or regulatory environment. You should also review your plans after any major disaster or near-miss to incorporate any lessons learned.

As a manager, you play a critical role in ensuring that your organization has effective disaster recovery and business continuity plans in place. You need to understand the importance of these plans and advocate for their implementation and ongoing maintenance.

You should also ensure that your team members are aware of their roles and responsibilities during a disaster and that they receive the necessary training. You should also work with your IT and other relevant departments to ensure that the necessary resources are in place to support disaster recovery and business continuity.

By taking an active role in disaster recovery and business continuity planning, you can help to ensure that your organization is prepared to withstand major disruptions, minimize downtime and data loss, and maintain the trust of your customers and stakeholders.

It's also important to consider the role of third-party vendors and service providers in your disaster recovery and business continuity plans. Many organizations rely on third parties for critical IT services, such as cloud hosting, data backup, and managed security services.

You need to ensure that your third-party vendors have adequate disaster recovery and business continuity plans in place and that these plans align with your own. You should review their plans, test them if possible, and ensure that they meet your RTO and RPO requirements.

You should also have contractual agreements in place with your third-party vendors that specify their responsibilities in the event of a disaster. These agreements should include service level agreements (SLAs) that define the expected level of service and the penalties for non-compliance.

Another important consideration is the location of your data backups and recovery sites. If you are using a cloud-based backup service or a remote data center, you need to consider the geographic location of these facilities.

Ideally, your backups and recovery sites should be located in a different geographic region than your primary data center. This helps to protect against regional disasters, such as earthquakes or hurricanes, that could affect both your primary and backup sites.

You should also consider the political and regulatory environment of the countries where your data is stored. Some countries have strict data privacy laws that could impact your ability to access or transfer your data in the event of a disaster.

In addition to technical measures, it's also important to have insurance coverage that can help to mitigate the financial impact of a disaster. This may include business interruption insurance, which covers lost income and expenses incurred during a disruption, and cyber insurance, which covers losses related to cyberattacks and data breaches.

When considering insurance coverage, it's important to understand the specific terms and conditions of each policy. You should also assess your organization's specific needs and risk profile to determine the appropriate level of coverage.

Disaster recovery and business continuity planning are not just about technology; they are also about people and processes. You need to have a well-defined organizational structure in place to manage a disaster, with clear roles and responsibilities.

You also need to have processes in place to ensure that your plans are regularly reviewed, updated, and tested. This requires ongoing commitment and resources from across the organization.

It's important to foster a culture of preparedness within your organization. This involves creating a shared sense of responsibility for disaster recovery and business continuity and encouraging employees to be proactive in identifying and mitigating risks.

By creating a culture of preparedness, you can empower your employees to be your first line of defense against disasters. They can help to identify potential risks, report incidents promptly, and respond effectively when a disaster occurs.

Disaster recovery and business continuity planning are essential components of any comprehensive cybersecurity program. They help to ensure that your organization can continue to operate or quickly resume operations in the face of a major disruption, minimizing downtime and data loss.

By conducting a thorough business impact analysis, determining your RTOs and RPOs, developing detailed recovery plans, regularly testing and updating your plans, and fostering a culture of preparedness, you can significantly improve your organization's resilience in the face of adversity.

While the specific steps involved in disaster recovery and business continuity planning will vary depending on your organization's unique needs and circumstances, the overall process remains the same. It's about understanding your risks, planning for the worst-case scenario, and being prepared to respond effectively when a disaster strikes.

As a manager, your leadership and support are vital to the success of your organization's disaster recovery and business continuity efforts. By prioritizing these efforts, allocating the necessary resources, and fostering a culture of preparedness, you can help to ensure that your organization is well-equipped to weather any storm and emerge stronger on the other side. It is a strategic investment in the long-term health and success of your business, demonstrating to stakeholders that you are prepared to meet the challenges of today and the uncertainties of tomorrow. This proactive approach to disaster recovery and business continuity is not just an IT responsibility; it's a business imperative that safeguards your operations, your reputation, and your future in an increasingly unpredictable world.

CHAPTER FIFTEEN: Vulnerability Management and Penetration Testing

In our ongoing exploration of cybersecurity, we've covered the essential elements of building a robust defense strategy, from understanding the threat landscape to implementing security frameworks and navigating the complexities of data protection regulations. We've fortified our networks, secured our endpoints, and addressed the unique challenges of the cloud. We've also empowered our employees through security awareness training and prepared for the inevitable with incident response, disaster recovery, and business continuity planning. Now, we turn our attention to a proactive approach to identifying and mitigating security weaknesses before they can be exploited by cybercriminals: vulnerability management and penetration testing.

Think of vulnerability management and penetration testing as the security equivalent of a regular health check-up and a stress test for your organization's digital infrastructure. Just as a doctor examines a patient for potential health issues and tests their physical limits, vulnerability management and penetration testing involve systematically examining your systems and networks for security weaknesses and simulating real-world attacks to assess your defenses.

Vulnerability management is the ongoing process of identifying, classifying, prioritizing, remediating, and mitigating vulnerabilities. Vulnerabilities are weaknesses in your systems, networks, or applications that could be exploited by attackers to gain unauthorized access, steal data, or disrupt operations. These weaknesses can be caused by various factors, such as software bugs, misconfigurations, outdated systems, or inadequate security controls.

Penetration testing, often referred to as "pen testing," is a simulated cyberattack on your systems and networks to evaluate their security. It's a controlled and authorized attempt to identify vulnerabilities that could be exploited by real attackers. Pen testing goes beyond automated vulnerability scanning by actively attempting to exploit vulnerabilities and demonstrate the potential impact of a successful attack.

The primary goal of vulnerability management and penetration testing is to proactively identify and address security weaknesses before they can be exploited by cybercriminals. It's about finding the holes in your armor and patching them before you're attacked. It's also about testing your defenses under realistic conditions to ensure that they can withstand a real-world attack.

Vulnerability management is not a one-time event; it's an ongoing process that requires continuous attention. New vulnerabilities are discovered daily, and your systems and networks are constantly changing as new software is installed, configurations are modified, and new devices are added. Therefore, it's essential to regularly scan your environment for vulnerabilities and to have a systematic process for addressing them.

The first step in vulnerability management is to identify the assets that need to be scanned. This includes all the systems, networks, and applications that are part of your digital infrastructure. It's important to maintain an up-to-date inventory of your assets so that you know what needs to be scanned and so that you don't overlook any critical systems.

Once you have identified your assets, the next step is to conduct vulnerability scans. Vulnerability scanning involves using automated tools to scan your systems and networks for known vulnerabilities. These tools compare your systems against a database of known vulnerabilities and generate a report that lists any vulnerabilities found.

There are many different vulnerability scanning tools available, both commercial and open-source. Some popular examples include Nessus, Qualys, and OpenVAS. These tools can scan a wide range of systems and applications, including operating systems, web servers, databases, and network devices.

Vulnerability scans can be conducted on a regular basis, such as weekly or monthly, or they can be conducted on-demand, such as after a new system is installed or a new vulnerability is discovered. It's important to schedule scans during off-peak hours to minimize the impact on your systems and network performance.

Once a vulnerability scan is complete, the next step is to classify and prioritize the vulnerabilities that were found. Not all vulnerabilities are created equal. Some vulnerabilities are more critical than others, depending on factors such as the severity of the vulnerability, the likelihood of it being exploited, and the potential impact of a successful exploit.

Vulnerability classification typically involves assigning a severity rating to each vulnerability. This rating is often based on the Common Vulnerability Scoring System (CVSS), which is an industry-standard method for assessing the severity of vulnerabilities. CVSS scores range from 0 to 10, with 10 being the most severe.

In addition to severity, it's also important to consider the likelihood of a vulnerability being exploited. This can depend on factors such as the availability of exploit code, the ease of exploitation, and the attacker's motivation. For example, a vulnerability that is publicly known and has exploit code readily available is more likely to be exploited than a vulnerability that is not well-known and requires specialized skills to exploit.

The potential impact of a successful exploit should also be considered when prioritizing vulnerabilities. This involves assessing the potential consequences if a particular vulnerability were to be exploited. The impact could be financial, operational, reputational, or legal. For example, a vulnerability that could allow an attacker to gain access to sensitive customer data would have a higher impact than a vulnerability that could only be used to cause a minor service disruption.

Once you have classified and prioritized your vulnerabilities, the next step is to remediate them. Remediation involves taking steps to address the vulnerabilities and reduce the risk of them being exploited. This may involve applying patches, changing configurations, or implementing other security controls.

The most common method of remediation is patching. Software vendors regularly release patches to fix vulnerabilities in their products. Applying these patches promptly is crucial for protecting your systems from known exploits.

However, patching can be a complex and time-consuming process, especially in large organizations with many different types of systems and applications. It requires careful planning, testing, and coordination to ensure that patches are applied correctly and do not cause any unintended consequences.

Automated patch management tools can help to streamline this process. These tools can automatically scan your systems for missing patches, download the patches from vendor websites, and deploy them to the appropriate systems.

In some cases, patching may not be possible or practical. For example, a patch may not be available for a particular vulnerability, or applying a patch may cause compatibility issues with other software. In these cases, you may need to implement other mitigating controls, such as changing configurations, implementing workarounds, or isolating affected systems.

After remediating vulnerabilities, it's important to verify that the remediation was successful. This can be done by conducting another vulnerability scan to ensure that the vulnerabilities are no longer present.

The final step in the vulnerability management process is to monitor your systems and networks for new vulnerabilities. This involves staying informed about the latest threats and vulnerabilities and regularly scanning your environment for new weaknesses.

Vulnerability management is an ongoing process that requires continuous attention and improvement. You should regularly review your vulnerability management program to ensure that it is effective and that it is keeping pace with the evolving threat landscape.

While vulnerability management is an essential part of any cybersecurity program, it is not sufficient on its own. Vulnerability scans can only identify known vulnerabilities; they cannot identify unknown vulnerabilities or assess the effectiveness of your security controls against real-world attacks. This is where penetration testing comes in.

Penetration testing is a simulated cyberattack on your systems and networks to evaluate their security. It's a controlled and authorized attempt to identify vulnerabilities that could be exploited by real attackers. Pen testing goes beyond automated vulnerability scanning by actively attempting to exploit vulnerabilities and demonstrate the potential impact of a successful attack.

The primary goal of penetration testing is to identify security weaknesses before they can be exploited by cybercriminals. It's about finding the holes in your armor and patching them before you're attacked. It's also about testing your defenses under realistic conditions to ensure that they can withstand a real-world attack.

Penetration testing can be conducted on various aspects of your digital infrastructure, including your networks, systems, applications, and even your employees through social engineering tests.

There are several different types of penetration testing, including:

- **External penetration testing:** This type of testing simulates an attack from outside your organization's network. It focuses on identifying vulnerabilities that could be exploited by an attacker who does not have physical access to your premises.

- **Internal penetration testing:** This type of testing simulates an attack from within your organization's network. It focuses on identifying vulnerabilities that could be exploited by an insider threat or by an attacker who has already gained access to your network.

- **Web application penetration testing:** This type of testing focuses on identifying vulnerabilities in your web applications. It involves testing the application's input validation, authentication, authorization, and session management mechanisms.

- **Wireless penetration testing:** This type of testing focuses on identifying vulnerabilities in your wireless networks. It involves testing the security of your Wi-Fi access points, encryption protocols, and authentication mechanisms.

- **Social engineering testing:** This type of testing focuses on assessing your employees' susceptibility to social engineering attacks, such as phishing. It involves sending simulated phishing emails or making phone calls to employees to test their ability to recognize and resist these attacks.

Penetration testing typically involves several phases, including:

- **Planning and reconnaissance:** In this phase, the penetration tester defines the scope and objectives of the test, gathers information about the target systems and networks, and identifies potential vulnerabilities.

- **Scanning:** In this phase, the penetration tester uses automated tools to scan the target systems and networks for open ports, running services, and known vulnerabilities.

- **Gaining access:** In this phase, the penetration tester attempts to exploit the identified vulnerabilities to gain unauthorized access to the target systems and networks.

- **Maintaining access:** In this phase, the penetration tester attempts to maintain access to the compromised systems and networks, often by installing backdoors or other persistence mechanisms.

- **Analysis and reporting:** In this phase, the penetration tester analyzes the results of the test, documents the findings, and provides recommendations for remediation.

Penetration testing should be conducted by qualified and experienced professionals. These professionals, often referred to as ethical hackers or white-hat hackers, have the skills and knowledge to simulate real-world attacks without causing harm to your systems or data.

It's important to choose a reputable penetration testing provider with a proven track record. You should also ensure that they have the appropriate certifications, such as Certified Ethical Hacker (CEH) or Offensive Security Certified Professional (OSCP).

Before conducting a penetration test, it's crucial to establish clear rules of engagement. These rules define the scope of the test, the systems and networks that will be tested, the types of attacks that will be used, and the time frame for the test. The rules of engagement should also specify any restrictions or limitations, such as systems or data that are off-limits.

It's also important to obtain written authorization from the appropriate stakeholders before conducting a penetration test. This helps to ensure that everyone is aware of the test and that there are no misunderstandings about its scope or objectives.

During the penetration test, the testing team should maintain regular communication with your organization's designated point of contact. This helps to ensure that the test is proceeding as planned and that any issues or concerns are addressed promptly.

After the penetration test is complete, the testing team should provide a detailed report that outlines their findings, including the vulnerabilities they identified, the methods they used to exploit them, and the potential impact of a successful attack. The report should also include recommendations for remediation.

It's important to carefully review the penetration testing report and to take prompt action to address the identified vulnerabilities. You should prioritize the vulnerabilities based on their severity, likelihood of exploitation, and potential impact, just as you would with vulnerabilities identified through vulnerability scanning.

Penetration testing should be conducted on a regular basis, such as annually or after any significant changes to your systems or networks. It's also a good idea to conduct penetration testing after implementing new security controls to ensure that they are effective.

In addition to regular penetration testing, it's also important to conduct targeted penetration tests when new threats or vulnerabilities emerge. For example, if a new type of attack is discovered that could potentially impact your systems, you may want to conduct a targeted penetration test to assess your vulnerability to that specific attack.

Vulnerability management and penetration testing are complementary activities that work together to provide a comprehensive assessment of your organization's security posture. Vulnerability scanning provides a broad overview of known vulnerabilities, while penetration testing provides a deeper, more realistic assessment of your defenses against real-world attacks.

By combining vulnerability management and penetration testing, you can gain a more complete understanding of your security weaknesses and take proactive steps to address them before they can be exploited by cybercriminals.

As a manager, you play a critical role in ensuring that your organization has effective vulnerability management and penetration testing programs in place. You need to understand the importance of these activities and advocate for their implementation and ongoing maintenance.

You should also ensure that your team members are aware of their roles and responsibilities in these processes. For example, your IT staff may be responsible for conducting vulnerability scans and implementing patches, while your security team may be responsible for overseeing penetration testing and analyzing the results.

It's also important to allocate sufficient resources to vulnerability management and penetration testing. This includes not only the budget for tools and services but also the staff time and expertise needed to effectively manage these programs.

By taking an active role in vulnerability management and penetration testing, you can help to ensure that your organization is proactively identifying and mitigating security weaknesses, reducing the risk of a successful cyberattack. These proactive measures are not just an IT responsibility; they are a business imperative that safeguards your operations, your reputation, and your future in the digital age. They demonstrate a commitment to security and resilience, showing stakeholders that you are taking the necessary steps to protect your organization from the ever-evolving threat landscape.

CHAPTER SIXTEEN: Secure Software Development Lifecycle

In our exploration of cybersecurity, we've covered the gamut from understanding the threat landscape and identifying digital assets to implementing security frameworks, navigating data protection regulations, and fortifying our defenses through network security, endpoint protection, cloud security, identity and access management, security awareness training, incident response planning, disaster recovery, and business continuity. We've also proactively addressed vulnerabilities through vulnerability management and penetration testing. Now, we turn our attention to a critical aspect of cybersecurity that underpins the security of the very applications and systems we rely on: the Secure Software Development Lifecycle (SSDLC).

The SSDLC is a process that integrates security into every stage of software development, from the initial planning and design phase to development, testing, deployment, and maintenance. It's about building security into software from the ground up, rather than trying to bolt it on as an afterthought. It's a proactive approach that aims to prevent vulnerabilities from being introduced in the first place, reducing the risk of security incidents and ensuring the confidentiality, integrity, and availability of the software and the data it handles.

Think of the SSDLC as a recipe for building secure software. Just as a chef carefully selects ingredients, follows a recipe, and tastes the dish at various stages to ensure it meets their standards, the SSDLC provides a structured approach to developing software with security as a core consideration at every step.

In today's digital landscape, software is ubiquitous. It powers our websites, mobile apps, business applications, and even critical infrastructure. As organizations increasingly rely on software to conduct their operations, the security of that software becomes paramount. A single vulnerability in an application can be exploited by attackers to gain unauthorized access, steal data, or disrupt operations, potentially causing significant financial, operational, and reputational damage.

Traditionally, security has often been treated as an afterthought in software development. Developers focused on functionality, performance, and usability, while security was often addressed late in the development process, if at all. This approach is no longer viable in today's threat environment. Security must be a primary consideration from the outset, integrated into every stage of the software development lifecycle.

The SSDLC is not a one-size-fits-all solution. There are various SSDLC models and frameworks available, each with its own specific steps and processes. However, they all share a common goal: to integrate security into every phase of software development.

One of the most widely recognized SSDLC models is the Microsoft Security Development Lifecycle. This model consists of seven phases: training, requirements, design, implementation, verification, release, and response.

The training phase focuses on educating developers, architects, and testers about secure coding practices, common vulnerabilities, and the latest security threats. This helps to build a security-aware culture within the development team and ensures that everyone understands their role in developing secure software.

The requirements phase involves defining security requirements for the software. This includes identifying the types of data the software will handle, the applicable regulatory requirements, and the potential threats the software may face. Security requirements should be documented and treated with the same level of importance as functional requirements.

The design phase involves designing the software architecture with security in mind. This includes identifying potential attack surfaces, defining security controls, and selecting appropriate security technologies. Threat modeling is a key activity in this phase. Threat modeling is a process for identifying and prioritizing potential threats to a system and determining the best way to mitigate those threats.

The implementation phase involves writing the code for the software, following secure coding practices. This includes validating input, handling errors properly, protecting sensitive data, and using secure libraries and frameworks. Code reviews are an important part of this phase. Code reviews involve having other developers examine the code for potential security vulnerabilities and coding errors.

The verification phase involves testing the software to ensure that it meets the defined security requirements and is free from vulnerabilities. This includes various types of security testing, such as static analysis, dynamic analysis, and penetration testing. Static analysis involves examining the code without executing it to identify potential vulnerabilities. Dynamic analysis involves testing the software while it is running to identify vulnerabilities. Penetration testing, as we discussed in the previous chapter, involves simulating real-world attacks to assess the security of the software.

The release phase involves preparing the software for deployment. This includes conducting a final security review, creating secure installation packages, and developing security documentation for users.

The response phase involves monitoring the software for security incidents and responding to any vulnerabilities that are discovered after the software has been released. This includes having a process for receiving vulnerability reports, verifying them, developing and releasing patches, and communicating with users about the vulnerabilities and the patches.

Another popular SSDLC framework is the OWASP Software Assurance Maturity Model (SAMM). OWASP SAMM is a framework for measuring and improving an organization's software security posture. It provides a set of best practices for integrating security into the software development lifecycle, organized into five business functions: governance, construction, verification, deployment, and operations.

Each business function contains three security practices. For example, the governance function includes the security practices of strategy and metrics, policy and compliance, and education and guidance. Each security practice is further broken down into activities, which are specific actions that organizations can take to improve their software security posture.

OWASP SAMM also includes a maturity model that allows organizations to assess their current level of software security maturity and set goals for improvement. The maturity model consists of four levels: initial, defined, managed, and optimized.

Regardless of which SSDLC model or framework you choose, the key is to integrate security into every stage of the software development lifecycle. This requires a cultural shift within the development team, where security is seen as a shared responsibility and not just the responsibility of the security team.

Implementing an SSDLC requires a commitment from all stakeholders, including developers, testers, project managers, and senior management. It requires establishing clear security policies and procedures, providing training to developers on secure coding practices, and using appropriate tools and technologies to support secure development.

One of the first steps in implementing an SSDLC is to define a security policy for software development. This policy should outline the organization's approach to secure development, including the roles and responsibilities of different stakeholders, the required security activities at each stage of the development lifecycle, and the metrics that will be used to measure the effectiveness of the SSDLC.

The policy should also define the acceptable level of risk for the software being developed. This involves considering factors such as the sensitivity of the data the software will handle, the potential impact of a security breach, and the applicable regulatory requirements.

Another important step is to provide training to developers on secure coding practices. This training should cover topics such as common vulnerabilities (e.g., those listed in the OWASP Top 10), secure coding techniques, and the use of security tools. The training should be tailored to the specific programming languages and technologies used by the development team.

In addition to training, it's also important to provide developers with access to secure coding guidelines and standards. These guidelines provide specific recommendations on how to write secure code for different programming languages and platforms. They can cover topics such as input validation, output encoding, error handling, authentication, authorization, session management, and cryptography.

Secure coding standards can be developed in-house or adopted from industry best practices, such as those provided by OWASP or CERT. It's important to ensure that the guidelines are kept up-to-date with the latest security threats and vulnerabilities.

Another key aspect of implementing an SSDLC is the use of appropriate tools and technologies to support secure development. This can include static analysis tools, dynamic analysis tools, and interactive application security testing (IAST) tools.

Static analysis tools, also known as static application security testing (SAST) tools, analyze source code or compiled code for potential security vulnerabilities without executing the code. They work by comparing the code against a set of rules or patterns that are known to be associated with vulnerabilities. SAST tools can identify a wide range of vulnerabilities, such as SQL injection, cross-site scripting (XSS), and buffer overflows.

Dynamic analysis tools, also known as dynamic application security testing (DAST) tools, test running applications for vulnerabilities by sending them various inputs and observing their responses. DAST tools can identify vulnerabilities that are difficult to detect with static analysis, such as authentication and session management issues.

IAST tools combine elements of both SAST and DAST to provide a more comprehensive analysis of application security. They instrument the application's runtime environment to monitor its behavior and identify vulnerabilities. IAST tools can provide more accurate results than SAST or DAST alone, with fewer false positives.

In addition to these testing tools, it's also important to use secure libraries and frameworks when developing software. These libraries and frameworks provide pre-built, security-tested components that can be used to perform common tasks, such as authentication, authorization, and encryption. Using secure libraries and frameworks can help to reduce the risk of introducing vulnerabilities into the software.

Another important aspect of the SSDLC is threat modeling. Threat modeling is a structured process for identifying and prioritizing potential threats to a system and determining the best way to mitigate those threats. It involves analyzing the system's architecture, identifying potential attack surfaces, and brainstorming potential threats.

Threat modeling should be conducted early in the development lifecycle, during the design phase. This allows security controls to be built into the system from the outset, rather than being added as an afterthought.

There are various threat modeling methodologies available, such as STRIDE, PASTA, and OCTAVE. STRIDE, which stands for Spoofing, Tampering, Repudiation, Information Disclosure, Denial of Service, and Elevation of Privilege, is a widely used methodology developed by Microsoft. It provides a framework for categorizing threats and identifying potential mitigations.

PASTA, which stands for Process for Attack Simulation and Threat Analysis, is a risk-centric threat modeling methodology that focuses on aligning business objectives with technical requirements. It involves seven stages, including defining objectives, defining the technical scope, application decomposition, threat analysis, vulnerability and weakness analysis, attack modeling, and risk and impact analysis.

OCTAVE, which stands for Operationally Critical Threat, Asset, and Vulnerability Evaluation, is a risk-based strategic assessment and planning technique for security. It is a self-directed approach, meaning that the organization itself is responsible for conducting the threat modeling process.

Regardless of which methodology you choose, the goal of threat modeling is to identify potential threats to the system and to determine the appropriate security controls to mitigate those threats. The output of the threat modeling process should be a prioritized list of threats and a set of security requirements that address those threats.

Another important aspect of the SSDLC is code review. Code review is the process of examining source code to identify potential security vulnerabilities, coding errors, and violations of coding standards. Code reviews can be conducted manually or using automated tools.

Manual code reviews involve having developers examine each other's code, looking for potential security issues. This can be a time-consuming process, but it can also be very effective, especially when conducted by experienced developers with a strong understanding of security.

Automated code review tools, such as static analysis tools, can help to streamline the code review process by automatically identifying potential vulnerabilities. However, automated tools are not a replacement for manual code reviews. They should be used in conjunction with manual reviews to provide a more comprehensive assessment of code security.

Code reviews should be conducted regularly throughout the development lifecycle, not just at the end. This helps to identify and address security issues early in the development process, when they are easier and less costly to fix.

In addition to code reviews, it's also important to conduct security testing throughout the development lifecycle. This includes unit testing, integration testing, and system testing.

Unit testing involves testing individual components of the software to ensure that they function as expected and are free from vulnerabilities. Integration testing involves testing the interactions between different components of the software to ensure that they work together correctly and securely. System testing involves testing the entire system to ensure that it meets the defined security requirements and is free from vulnerabilities.

Security testing should not be limited to functional testing. It should also include non-functional testing, such as performance testing and load testing, to ensure that the software can handle expected loads and does not become vulnerable under stress.

Another important aspect of the SSDLC is secure deployment. Secure deployment involves ensuring that the software is deployed in a secure manner to a secure environment. This includes configuring the production environment with appropriate security controls, such as firewalls, intrusion detection systems, and access controls.

It's also important to ensure that the software is installed and configured securely. This includes using secure installation packages, disabling unnecessary services and features, and configuring the software with strong security settings.

Once the software has been deployed, it's important to monitor it for security incidents and to respond to any vulnerabilities that are discovered. This involves having a process for receiving vulnerability reports, verifying them, developing and releasing patches, and communicating with users about the vulnerabilities and the patches.

Implementing an SSDLC is not a one-time project; it's an ongoing process that requires continuous improvement. You should regularly review your SSDLC processes and procedures to ensure that they are effective and that they are keeping pace with the evolving threat landscape.

This may involve conducting regular assessments of your software security posture, measuring the effectiveness of your SSDLC using metrics, and making adjustments to your processes and procedures based on the results of these assessments.

Metrics can be a valuable tool for measuring the effectiveness of your SSDLC. There are various metrics that can be used, such as the number of vulnerabilities identified during development, the number of vulnerabilities identified after release, the time it takes to remediate vulnerabilities, and the number of security incidents related to software vulnerabilities.

By tracking these metrics over time, you can identify trends, measure the impact of your SSDLC efforts, and make data-driven decisions about how to improve your software security posture.

As a manager, you play a crucial role in ensuring that your organization adopts and effectively implements an SSDLC. You need to understand the importance of secure software development and advocate for its integration into your organization's development processes.

You should also ensure that your development teams receive the necessary training, tools, and resources to implement the SSDLC. This may involve working with your IT and security teams to define security requirements, select appropriate tools, and establish secure coding standards.

It's also important to foster a culture of security awareness within your development teams. This involves creating a shared sense of responsibility for security and encouraging developers to be proactive in identifying and addressing security issues.

By taking an active role in promoting and supporting the SSDLC, you can help to ensure that your organization develops secure, high-quality software that meets the needs of your business and protects your customers' data.

The benefits of implementing an SSDLC are numerous. First and foremost, it significantly reduces the risk of security vulnerabilities in your software. By integrating security into every stage of the development lifecycle, you can prevent vulnerabilities from being introduced in the first place and catch those that do slip through early in the process, when they are easier and less costly to fix.

An SSDLC also helps to improve the overall quality of your software. By focusing on security, you are also focusing on reliability, maintainability, and other quality attributes that are essential for building robust, high-performing software.

Moreover, an SSDLC can help you achieve and maintain compliance with various regulations and standards, such as the GDPR, HIPAA, and PCI DSS. These regulations often require organizations to demonstrate that they have implemented appropriate security measures to protect sensitive data, and an SSDLC can provide evidence of such measures.

Implementing an SSDLC can also lead to cost savings in the long run. While there may be upfront costs associated with training, tools, and process changes, these costs are typically far outweighed by the potential costs of a security breach, such as incident response, legal fees, regulatory fines, and reputational damage.

Furthermore, an SSDLC can enhance your organization's reputation and build trust with your customers. By demonstrating your commitment to developing secure software, you can differentiate yourself from competitors and show your customers that you take their security seriously.

The Secure Software Development Lifecycle is a critical component of any comprehensive cybersecurity program. It's about building security into software from the ground up, rather than trying to bolt it on as an afterthought. By integrating security into every stage of the development process, you can significantly reduce the risk of security vulnerabilities, improve the overall quality of your software, achieve compliance with regulations, save costs, and enhance your reputation. While implementing an SSDLC requires a commitment from all stakeholders and a cultural shift within the development team, the benefits far outweigh the challenges. As a manager, your leadership and support are vital to the success of your organization's SSDLC efforts, ensuring that security is a primary consideration throughout the software development journey. This proactive approach to secure development is not just an IT responsibility; it's a business imperative that safeguards your operations, your reputation, and your future in an increasingly interconnected and software-dependent world.

CHAPTER SEVENTEEN: Third-Party Risk Management

In our exploration of cybersecurity's multifaceted landscape, we've delved into understanding threats, identifying assets, assessing risks, building strategies, implementing frameworks, navigating data protection regulations, and fortifying defenses across networks, endpoints, and cloud environments. We've empowered employees through training, prepared for incidents with robust response plans, ensured business continuity, and proactively managed vulnerabilities while integrating security into our software development lifecycle. Now, we address a critical aspect of cybersecurity that extends beyond the boundaries of your organization: third-party risk management (TPRM).

In today's interconnected world, businesses rarely operate in isolation. They rely on a vast network of third-party vendors, suppliers, contractors, and partners to provide essential services, support operations, and drive growth. These third parties often have access to sensitive data, systems, and networks, creating a complex web of interdependencies that can significantly impact an organization's security posture.

Think of third-party risk management as extending your cybersecurity perimeter to encompass your entire ecosystem. It's about recognizing that your organization's security is only as strong as the weakest link in your supply chain. A vulnerability or security lapse in a third-party's environment can have direct and potentially devastating consequences for your business, even if your own defenses are robust.

Third-party risk management is the process of identifying, assessing, mitigating, and monitoring the risks associated with your third-party relationships. It's about understanding the potential threats that these relationships pose to your organization and taking proactive steps to address them. It's not about eliminating all third-party relationships; it's about managing the risks they introduce in a systematic and informed manner.

The primary goal of TPRM is to ensure that your third-party relationships do not compromise your organization's security, compliance, or operational resilience. It's about extending your security policies, standards, and controls to your third parties and holding them accountable for maintaining an appropriate level of security.

The importance of TPRM has grown exponentially in recent years, driven by several factors. First, the increasing reliance on third parties for critical business functions has expanded the attack surface, providing more opportunities for cybercriminals to exploit vulnerabilities. Second, high-profile data breaches involving third parties have highlighted the devastating consequences of inadequate TPRM, damaging reputations and eroding customer trust. Third, regulatory bodies around the world are increasingly scrutinizing organizations' third-party risk management practices, imposing stricter requirements and penalties for non-compliance.

One of the first steps in implementing a TPRM program is to identify all your third-party relationships. This may seem like a simple task, but it can be surprisingly complex, especially in large organizations with decentralized procurement processes. You need to create a comprehensive inventory of all your vendors, suppliers, contractors, and partners, including those that have access to your sensitive data, systems, or networks.

This inventory should include not only your direct, or "tier-one," third parties but also their subcontractors and other downstream vendors, sometimes referred to as "nth parties." This is because vulnerabilities in these downstream relationships can also pose a risk to your organization, even if you don't have a direct relationship with them.

Once you have identified your third parties, the next step is to assess the risks associated with each relationship. This involves evaluating the criticality of the services provided by the third party, the sensitivity of the data they handle, the security controls they have in place, and their compliance with relevant regulations.

Risk assessments should be conducted based on a consistent and objective methodology. This may involve using questionnaires, reviewing security documentation, conducting on-site assessments, and leveraging third-party risk intelligence services. The goal is to gain a clear understanding of each third party's security posture and to identify any gaps or weaknesses that need to be addressed.

Not all third-party relationships pose the same level of risk. A vendor that provides office supplies, for example, is likely to pose a lower risk than a cloud service provider that stores and processes your sensitive customer data. Therefore, it's important to prioritize your risk assessments based on the criticality of the relationship and the potential impact of a security incident.

Once you have assessed the risks, the next step is to determine the appropriate level of due diligence for each third party. Due diligence is the process of investigating and verifying the security practices of a third party before entering into a relationship with them. The level of due diligence should be commensurate with the level of risk posed by the relationship.

For low-risk relationships, due diligence may involve a simple questionnaire and a review of publicly available information. For higher-risk relationships, it may involve more in-depth assessments, such as on-site audits, penetration testing, and reviews of security certifications, such as ISO 27001 or SOC 2.

The results of your risk assessments and due diligence should inform your decisions about whether to enter into a relationship with a particular third party, what security requirements to include in your contracts, and what ongoing monitoring activities are necessary.

Contractual agreements play a crucial role in third-party risk management. Your contracts with third parties should clearly define the security requirements and expectations for the relationship. This includes specifying the security standards that the third party must adhere to, the types of security assessments they must undergo, and their obligations in the event of a security incident.

Your contracts should also include provisions for ongoing monitoring and auditing of the third party's security posture. This may involve requiring the third party to provide regular security reports, to undergo periodic security assessments, or to allow your organization to conduct audits of their security controls.

In addition to contractual requirements, it's also important to establish clear communication channels with your third parties. This includes defining points of contact for security-related issues, establishing procedures for reporting and responding to security incidents, and conducting regular meetings to discuss security performance and address any concerns.

Ongoing monitoring is a critical component of TPRM. The security landscape is constantly evolving, and a third party's security posture can change over time. Therefore, it's essential to continuously monitor your third-party relationships to ensure that they continue to meet your security requirements.

Ongoing monitoring may involve various activities, such as reviewing security reports provided by the third party, conducting periodic risk assessments, monitoring threat intelligence feeds for information about your third parties, and tracking their compliance with contractual obligations.

Automation can play a significant role in streamlining and improving the effectiveness of ongoing monitoring. There are various TPRM software solutions available that can automate tasks such as risk assessments, due diligence, and continuous monitoring. These solutions can help you manage your third-party relationships more efficiently and provide you with real-time visibility into your third-party risk landscape.

In addition to monitoring your existing third-party relationships, it's also important to have a process in place for evaluating the security of new third parties before engaging with them. This involves conducting due diligence as part of the procurement process and ensuring that security requirements are incorporated into contracts from the outset.

Managing third-party risk is not just an IT or security function; it requires collaboration across multiple departments, including procurement, legal, compliance, and business units. Each of these departments plays a role in identifying, assessing, and managing third-party risks.

Procurement is often the first point of contact with potential third parties. They should be trained to identify potential security risks during the vendor selection process and to involve the security team in evaluating the security posture of potential vendors.

Legal is responsible for ensuring that contracts with third parties include appropriate security requirements and that these requirements are enforceable. They should also be involved in any legal issues that arise related to third-party security incidents.

Compliance is responsible for ensuring that your organization's third-party risk management practices comply with relevant regulations and industry standards. They should also be involved in assessing the compliance of your third parties with these regulations and standards.

Business units are often the "owners" of third-party relationships. They should be involved in identifying the risks associated with these relationships and in ensuring that the third parties they work with are meeting the organization's security requirements.

As a manager, you play a crucial role in ensuring that your organization has an effective TPRM program in place. You need to understand the importance of managing third-party risk and advocate for the implementation of appropriate policies, procedures, and controls.

You should also ensure that your team members are aware of their responsibilities related to third-party risk management and that they receive the necessary training. This includes understanding the organization's TPRM policies, knowing how to identify and report potential security risks associated with third parties, and understanding their role in any incident response procedures involving third parties.

It's also important to foster a culture of security awareness that extends to your third-party relationships. This involves creating a shared sense of responsibility for security and encouraging open communication about security issues, both internally and with your third parties.

By taking an active role in promoting and supporting TPRM, you can help to ensure that your organization is effectively managing the risks associated with its third-party relationships, protecting its sensitive data, and maintaining the trust of its customers and partners.

The benefits of a well-implemented TPRM program are numerous. First and foremost, it significantly reduces the risk of security incidents involving third parties. By identifying and mitigating vulnerabilities in your third-party ecosystem, you can prevent data breaches, operational disruptions, and other security incidents that could harm your organization.

A strong TPRM program also helps to ensure compliance with various regulations and industry standards. Many regulations, such as the GDPR and the CCPA, require organizations to manage the risks associated with their third-party relationships. By implementing a robust TPRM program, you can demonstrate compliance with these regulations and avoid potential penalties.

Moreover, an effective TPRM program can enhance your organization's overall security posture. By extending your security policies, standards, and controls to your third parties, you can create a more consistent and comprehensive approach to security across your entire ecosystem.

TPRM can also lead to cost savings in the long run. While there may be upfront costs associated with implementing a TPRM program, these costs are typically far outweighed by the potential costs of a security incident involving a third party. By proactively managing third-party risk, you can avoid the financial losses, legal fees, regulatory fines, and reputational damage that can result from such incidents.

Furthermore, a strong TPRM program can enhance your organization's reputation and build trust with your customers and partners. By demonstrating your commitment to managing third-party risk, you can differentiate yourself from competitors and show your stakeholders that you take their security seriously.

Third-party risk management is a critical component of any comprehensive cybersecurity program. It's about extending your security perimeter to encompass your entire ecosystem and ensuring that your third-party relationships do not compromise your organization's security, compliance, or operational resilience. By implementing a robust TPRM program, you can significantly reduce the risk of security incidents involving third parties, protect your sensitive data, and maintain the trust of your customers and partners. While implementing a TPRM program requires a commitment from all stakeholders and a collaborative approach across multiple departments, the benefits far outweigh the challenges. As a manager, your leadership and support are vital to the success of your organization's TPRM efforts, ensuring that third-party risk is managed effectively and that security is a primary consideration in all your third-party relationships. This proactive approach to managing third-party risk is not just an IT or security responsibility; it's a business imperative that safeguards your operations, your reputation, and your future in an increasingly interconnected world.

CHAPTER EIGHTEEN: The Role of Encryption

In the digital age, where data is the lifeblood of businesses, protecting sensitive information from unauthorized access and theft has become paramount. Encryption stands as a cornerstone of data security, serving as a powerful tool to safeguard digital assets. This chapter delves into the crucial role of encryption in cybersecurity, exploring its fundamental concepts, various types, and practical applications in business environments.

Encryption is the process of converting information into a code to prevent unauthorized access. It transforms readable data, known as plaintext, into an unreadable format called ciphertext. Only those with the proper decryption key can convert the ciphertext back into plaintext, ensuring that even if unauthorized parties intercept the data, they cannot understand or use it.

The concept of encryption dates back thousands of years, with early examples including the Caesar cipher used in ancient Rome. However, modern encryption has evolved far beyond these simple substitution ciphers, employing complex mathematical algorithms that make it virtually impossible to decrypt without the correct key.

In today's digital landscape, encryption plays a vital role in protecting various types of data, including:

1. Communication data: Emails, instant messages, and voice calls

2. Stored data: Files on computers, servers, and cloud storage

3. Transmitted data: Information sent over networks, including the internet

4. Financial transactions: Online banking and e-commerce activities

Encryption serves several critical functions in cybersecurity:

- Confidentiality: Encryption ensures that only authorized parties can access and understand the information.

- Integrity: Some encryption methods can detect if data has been tampered with during transmission or storage.

- Authentication: Encryption can be used to verify the identity of the sender or source of information.

- Non-repudiation: In some cases, encryption can provide proof that a specific user sent a message or performed an action.

There are two main types of encryption: symmetric and asymmetric. Symmetric encryption, also known as secret key encryption, uses the same key for both encryption and decryption. This method is fast and efficient, making it suitable for encrypting large amounts of data. However, the challenge lies in securely sharing the encryption key between parties.

Common symmetric encryption algorithms include:

1. Advanced Encryption Standard (AES): Widely used and considered highly secure, AES is employed in various applications, from securing Wi-Fi networks to protecting sensitive government information.

2. Data Encryption Standard (DES): An older algorithm that has been largely replaced by more secure options.

3. Twofish: A highly secure algorithm that was a finalist in the competition to select AES.

Asymmetric encryption, also called public key cryptography, uses a pair of keys: a public key for encryption and a private key for decryption. The public key can be freely shared, while the private key must be kept secret. This method addresses the key distribution problem of symmetric encryption and provides additional features like digital signatures.

Popular asymmetric encryption algorithms include:

1. RSA (Rivest-Shamir-Adleman): Widely used for secure data transmission and digital signatures.

2. Elliptic Curve Cryptography (ECC): Offers comparable security to RSA with shorter key lengths, making it more efficient.

3. Diffie-Hellman: Primarily used for secure key exchange over an insecure channel.

In practice, many systems use a combination of symmetric and asymmetric encryption. For example, asymmetric encryption might be used to securely exchange a symmetric key, which is then used for bulk data encryption due to its higher efficiency.

Encryption finds application in numerous areas of business cybersecurity:

1. Email Encryption: Businesses often need to exchange sensitive information via email. Email encryption ensures that even if an unauthorized party intercepts the message, they cannot read its contents. Popular email encryption standards include S/MIME (Secure/Multipurpose Internet Mail Extensions) and PGP (Pretty Good Privacy).

2. File and Disk Encryption: Encrypting files and entire disk drives protects data at rest. This is particularly important for mobile devices like laptops and smartphones, which are at risk of being lost or stolen. Full disk encryption (FDE) tools like BitLocker for Windows and FileVault for macOS provide this protection.

3. Database Encryption: Businesses store vast amounts of sensitive data in databases. Encrypting this data adds an extra layer of security, protecting against unauthorized

access even if the database is compromised. Many database management systems offer built-in encryption features.

4. Network Encryption: Data in transit over networks, especially public networks like the internet, is vulnerable to interception. Protocols like TLS (Transport Layer Security) and its predecessor SSL (Secure Sockets Layer) encrypt data as it travels across networks, forming the basis for HTTPS (Hypertext Transfer Protocol Secure) used in secure web browsing.

5. Virtual Private Networks (VPNs): VPNs use encryption to create a secure tunnel between a user's device and the company network, allowing remote workers to securely access company resources.

6. Cloud Storage Encryption: As businesses increasingly rely on cloud services, encrypting data before uploading it to the cloud (client-side encryption) ensures that even the cloud provider cannot access the unencrypted data.

7. Blockchain Technology: Encryption plays a crucial role in blockchain, the technology behind cryptocurrencies and other decentralized applications, ensuring the integrity and security of transactions.

While encryption is a powerful tool, its implementation comes with several considerations and challenges:

1. Key Management: Proper management of encryption keys is crucial. If keys are lost, encrypted data becomes inaccessible. If keys are compromised, the security of the encrypted data is at risk. Businesses need robust key management systems to generate, distribute, store, and retire encryption keys securely.

2. Performance Impact: Encryption and decryption processes require computational resources, which can impact system performance. This is particularly noticeable in high-volume

data processing scenarios. Businesses need to balance security needs with performance requirements.

3. Compliance Requirements: Various regulations, such as the General Data Protection Regulation (GDPR) and the Health Insurance Portability and Accountability Act (HIPAA), have specific requirements regarding data encryption. Businesses need to ensure their encryption practices comply with relevant regulations.

4. Encryption Backdoors: There's ongoing debate about whether encryption systems should include backdoors for law enforcement access. While this could aid in criminal investigations, it also introduces vulnerabilities that could be exploited by malicious actors.

5. Quantum Computing Threat: The advent of quantum computing poses a potential threat to many current encryption methods. Quantum computers could potentially break some widely used encryption algorithms, necessitating the development of quantum-resistant encryption methods.

6. User Experience: Strong encryption can sometimes lead to a more complex user experience. For example, users might need to manage multiple keys or passwords. Striking a balance between security and usability is crucial for widespread adoption of encryption technologies.

7. Encryption of Data in Use: While encryption of data at rest and in transit is well-established, protecting data while it's being processed (data in use) remains a challenge. Homomorphic encryption, which allows computations on encrypted data without decrypting it, is an emerging solution to this problem.

As businesses implement encryption strategies, several best practices should be followed:

1. Use Strong Encryption Algorithms: Always use well-established, publicly reviewed encryption algorithms. Avoid proprietary or custom encryption methods, as these have not undergone the same level of scrutiny and may contain unknown vulnerabilities.

2. Implement Proper Key Management: Use robust key management systems to securely generate, store, and rotate encryption keys. Consider using hardware security modules (HSMs) for added protection of cryptographic keys.

3. Encrypt Data at Rest and in Transit: Implement both file/disk encryption for stored data and network encryption for data in transit. This provides comprehensive protection for data throughout its lifecycle.

4. Regular Security Audits: Conduct regular audits of your encryption implementations to ensure they remain effective and up-to-date. This includes reviewing encryption policies, key management practices, and the strength of encryption algorithms in use.

5. Train Employees: Ensure that employees understand the importance of encryption and how to use encryption tools correctly. This is particularly important for email encryption and encrypted file sharing.

6. Plan for Key Recovery: Implement a secure process for key recovery in case encryption keys are lost. This prevents data loss due to inaccessible encrypted information.

7. Stay Informed: Keep abreast of developments in encryption technology and emerging threats. Be prepared to update your encryption strategies as new technologies and vulnerabilities come to light.

8. Consider Data Classification: Not all data requires the same level of encryption. Implement a data classification

scheme to determine appropriate encryption levels for different types of data.

9. Test Encryption Implementation: Regularly test your encryption implementation to ensure it's working as expected. This includes verifying that data is actually being encrypted and that it can be successfully decrypted when needed.

10. Integrate with Other Security Measures: While encryption is powerful, it should be part of a comprehensive security strategy that includes other measures like access controls, intrusion detection systems, and regular security training.

As encryption technologies continue to evolve, several trends are shaping the future of data protection:

1. Post-Quantum Cryptography: With the looming threat of quantum computers, there's increasing focus on developing encryption methods that can withstand quantum attacks. The National Institute of Standards and Technology (NIST) is in the process of standardizing post-quantum cryptographic algorithms.

2. Homomorphic Encryption: This technology allows computations to be performed on encrypted data without decrypting it. While currently computationally intensive, advancements in this field could revolutionize cloud computing security.

3. Blockchain-Based Encryption: The principles of blockchain technology are being applied to create decentralized, tamper-resistant encryption systems.

4. AI and Machine Learning in Cryptography: Artificial intelligence and machine learning are being explored for their potential to enhance encryption methods and detect cryptographic vulnerabilities.

5. Lightweight Cryptography: As Internet of Things (IoT) devices proliferate, there's a growing need for encryption methods that can work efficiently on devices with limited computational resources.

6. Quantum Key Distribution (QKD): This technology uses principles of quantum mechanics to securely distribute encryption keys, potentially providing unbreakable encryption.

Encryption serves as a critical line of defense in the ever-evolving landscape of cybersecurity. As data breaches and cyber attacks become increasingly sophisticated and frequent, the importance of robust encryption in protecting sensitive business information cannot be overstated. By understanding the principles of encryption, implementing best practices, and staying informed about emerging trends, businesses can significantly enhance their cybersecurity posture and protect their valuable digital assets.

CHAPTER NINETEEN: Mobile Security Best Practices

In today's interconnected business landscape, mobile devices have become indispensable tools for productivity and communication. Smartphones, tablets, and laptops allow employees to work from anywhere, at any time, enhancing flexibility and efficiency. However, this increased mobility also introduces significant security risks that businesses must address. This chapter explores the unique challenges of mobile security and provides best practices for managers to protect their organization's data and assets in an increasingly mobile world.

The proliferation of mobile devices in the workplace has blurred the lines between personal and professional use. Many employees use their personal devices for work purposes, a practice known as Bring Your Own Device (BYOD). While BYOD can reduce costs and increase employee satisfaction, it also complicates the task of securing corporate data and maintaining compliance with regulations.

Mobile devices face a variety of security threats, including:

1. Data loss or theft: Mobile devices are easily lost or stolen, potentially exposing sensitive corporate data.

2. Malware: Mobile devices are susceptible to malicious software, including viruses, trojans, and spyware.

3. Unsecured networks: Connecting to public Wi-Fi networks can expose devices to man-in-the-middle attacks and data interception.

4. Phishing attacks: Mobile users are often more vulnerable to phishing attempts due to the smaller screen size and limited security indicators on mobile browsers.

5. App-based threats: Malicious apps can compromise device security and access sensitive data.

6. Operating system vulnerabilities: Unpatched mobile operating systems can contain security flaws that attackers can exploit.

To address these threats and protect your organization's mobile assets, consider implementing the following best practices:

- Develop a comprehensive mobile security policy:

A well-defined mobile security policy is the foundation of any effective mobile security strategy. This policy should outline acceptable use guidelines, security requirements, and procedures for managing mobile devices. Key elements of a mobile security policy include:

4. Defining which devices and operating systems are allowed for business use

5. Establishing requirements for device passwords and lock screens

6. Outlining procedures for reporting lost or stolen devices

7. Specifying which apps are allowed or prohibited on devices used for work

8. Detailing data backup and synchronization procedures

9. Establishing guidelines for connecting to public Wi-Fi networks

10. Defining procedures for remote wiping of devices in case of loss or theft

Ensure that all employees are familiar with the mobile security policy and understand their responsibilities in protecting company data.

4. Implement Mobile Device Management (MDM) solutions:

Mobile Device Management software provides centralized control over mobile devices used within your organization. MDM solutions allow IT administrators to:

8. Enforce security policies across all devices

9. Configure and update device settings remotely

10.   Monitor device compliance with security policies

11.   Remotely lock or wipe lost or stolen devices

12.   Manage app installations and updates

13.   Separate personal and corporate data on devices

When selecting an MDM solution, consider factors such as compatibility with your existing IT infrastructure, ease of use, and the level of control it provides over different types of devices and operating systems.

8. Enforce strong authentication measures:

Implement multi-factor authentication (MFA) for accessing corporate resources from mobile devices. MFA requires users to provide two or more forms of identification before granting access, significantly reducing the risk of unauthorized access even if passwords are compromised.

Encourage the use of biometric authentication methods, such as fingerprint or facial recognition, where available. These methods are often more convenient for users and can be more secure than traditional passwords.

11.   Encrypt sensitive data:

Implement encryption for data stored on mobile devices and for data transmitted between mobile devices and corporate networks.

Use strong encryption algorithms and ensure that encryption keys are properly managed and protected.

For iOS devices, enable built-in encryption by requiring a passcode. For Android devices, enable full-disk encryption in the device settings. Additionally, use VPNs (Virtual Private Networks) to encrypt data transmitted over public Wi-Fi networks.

7. Regularly update and patch mobile devices:

Ensure that all mobile devices used for work purposes are running the latest version of their operating system and have all security patches installed. Unpatched devices can contain vulnerabilities that attackers can exploit to gain unauthorized access.

Consider implementing an automated patch management system as part of your MDM solution to ensure that all devices are kept up to date.

1. Control app installations:

Implement controls over which apps can be installed on devices used for work purposes. This can be achieved through:

- Creating a list of approved apps that employees are allowed to use for work

- Implementing an enterprise app store that only contains approved apps

- Using MDM solutions to block the installation of unapproved apps

Regularly review and update the list of approved apps to ensure it meets the changing needs of your organization while maintaining security.

1. Provide security awareness training:

Educate employees about mobile security risks and best practices. Training should cover topics such as:

- Recognizing and avoiding phishing attacks on mobile devices

- The importance of using strong, unique passwords

- How to securely connect to public Wi-Fi networks

- The risks associated with jailbreaking or rooting devices

- How to identify and report suspicious apps or activities

Regular training sessions and ongoing communication about mobile security can help reinforce the importance of following security best practices.

1. Implement secure communication channels:

Provide employees with secure messaging and file-sharing applications for work-related communications. These apps should use end-to-end encryption to protect the confidentiality of messages and files.

Discourage the use of personal messaging apps or unsecured email for sharing sensitive business information.

1. Develop a robust incident response plan:

Create a plan for responding to mobile security incidents, such as lost or stolen devices, malware infections, or data breaches. This plan should include:

- Procedures for reporting incidents

- Steps for containing and mitigating the impact of an incident

- Guidelines for communicating with affected parties

- Processes for investigating the cause of the incident and implementing preventive measures

Regularly test and update your incident response plan to ensure it remains effective in the face of evolving threats.

1. Monitor and audit mobile device usage:

Implement monitoring and auditing processes to track how mobile devices are being used within your organization. This can help identify potential security risks and ensure compliance with your mobile security policies.

Use MDM solutions and other security tools to collect and analyze data on device usage, app installations, and network connections. Regularly review this data to identify any anomalies or suspicious activities that may indicate a security threat.

1. Secure mobile app development:

If your organization develops mobile apps for internal use or for customers, implement secure coding practices throughout the development lifecycle. This includes:

- Conducting security assessments and penetration testing of mobile apps before deployment

- Implementing secure authentication and authorization mechanisms within apps

- Encrypting sensitive data stored or transmitted by the app

- Regularly updating and patching mobile apps to address any discovered vulnerabilities

- Consider mobile threat defense solutions:

In addition to MDM, consider implementing mobile threat defense (MTD) solutions. These tools provide real-time protection against mobile threats by:

- Detecting and blocking malicious apps

- Identifying network-based threats

- Monitoring for device vulnerabilities and configuration issues

- Providing visibility into mobile risks across your organization

MTD solutions can complement MDM and other security measures to provide a more comprehensive mobile security strategy.

1. Implement data loss prevention (DLP) for mobile devices:

Deploy DLP solutions that extend to mobile devices to prevent unauthorized sharing or leakage of sensitive data. DLP tools can:

- Monitor and control the transfer of sensitive data to and from mobile devices

- Prevent the copying or sharing of confidential information through unauthorized apps

- Enforce policies for handling sensitive data on mobile devices

- Manage mobile peripherals and IoT devices:

Consider the security implications of mobile peripherals and Internet of Things (IoT) devices that may connect to mobile devices used for work. Implement policies and technical controls to manage the use of:

- Bluetooth devices

- NFC (Near Field Communication) technology

- USB connections

- Wearable devices

Ensure that these connections do not introduce additional security risks to your mobile ecosystem.

1. Plan for device retirement and disposal:

Develop\procedures for securely retiring and disposing of mobile devices that are no longer needed or have reached the end of their lifecycle. This should include:

- Securely wiping all data from devices before disposal or reassignment

- Removing devices from MDM systems and revoking any associated access privileges

- Properly disposing of devices in compliance with environmental regulations

- Regularly assess and update your mobile security strategy:

The mobile threat landscape is constantly evolving, with new vulnerabilities and attack methods emerging regularly. To maintain an effective mobile security posture, it's crucial to:

- Conduct regular risk assessments to identify new threats and vulnerabilities

- Stay informed about the latest mobile security trends and best practices

- Periodically review and update your mobile security policies and procedures

- Evaluate the effectiveness of your current security controls and consider new technologies or solutions as needed

By implementing these mobile security best practices, organizations can significantly reduce the risks associated with mobile device use in the workplace. However, it's important to remember that mobile security is an ongoing process that requires continuous attention and adaptation.

As mobile technology continues to evolve, new security challenges will inevitably arise. Emerging technologies such as 5G networks, foldable devices, and advanced augmented reality applications will bring new opportunities for productivity and innovation, but also new security considerations.

To stay ahead of these challenges, organizations must foster a culture of security awareness among their employees and maintain a proactive approach to mobile security. This involves not only implementing technical controls but also promoting responsible mobile device use and empowering employees to make security-conscious decisions in their day-to-day work.

Managers play a crucial role in driving the adoption of mobile security best practices within their teams. By leading by example, enforcing security policies consistently, and emphasizing the importance of mobile security in team meetings and communications, managers can help create a security-minded culture that extends beyond the office and into the mobile workspace.

In conclusion, mobile security is no longer just an IT concern; it's a critical business imperative that requires attention and commitment from all levels of the organization. By implementing these best practices and maintaining a proactive approach to mobile security, businesses can harness the full potential of mobile technology while protecting their valuable data and assets from ever-evolving threats.

CHAPTER TWENTY: The Internet of Things (IoT) Security

The Internet of Things (IoT) has emerged as a transformative force in the business world, offering unprecedented opportunities for efficiency, innovation, and growth. However, as organizations increasingly adopt IoT devices and systems, they also face new and complex security challenges. This chapter explores the unique security considerations associated with IoT and provides managers with essential knowledge to navigate this rapidly evolving landscape.

IoT refers to the network of physical devices, vehicles, home appliances, and other items embedded with electronics, software, sensors, and network connectivity, which enables these objects to collect and exchange data. In a business context, IoT can include everything from smart thermostats and security cameras to industrial control systems and connected vehicles.

The proliferation of IoT devices in the workplace has brought numerous benefits, including:

1. Improved operational efficiency through real-time monitoring and automation

2. Enhanced data collection and analysis for better decision-making

3. Increased productivity through smart office environments

4. Reduced energy consumption and maintenance costs

5. Improved customer experiences through personalized services

However, the rapid adoption of IoT has also introduced significant security risks that organizations must address. Some of the key security challenges associated with IoT include:

- Expanded attack surface: Each IoT device represents a potential entry point for attackers, significantly expanding the attack surface of an organization's network.

- Device vulnerabilities: Many IoT devices lack basic security features, such as the ability to update firmware or change default passwords, making them easy targets for attackers.

- Data privacy concerns: IoT devices often collect and transmit sensitive data, raising concerns about data privacy and compliance with regulations such as GDPR and CCPA.

- Lack of standardization: The IoT landscape is fragmented, with numerous protocols and standards, making it challenging to implement consistent security measures across all devices.

- Scale and complexity: The sheer number of IoT devices and the complexity of IoT ecosystems can make it difficult to monitor and manage security effectively.

- Limited computing power: Many IoT devices have limited processing power and memory, making it challenging to implement robust security measures directly on the devices.

- Physical security: IoT devices are often deployed in physically accessible locations, making them vulnerable to tampering or theft.

To address these challenges and secure IoT deployments, organizations should consider implementing the following best practices:

11.   Conduct a thorough risk assessment: Before deploying IoT devices, conduct a comprehensive risk assessment to identify potential vulnerabilities and threats.

This assessment should consider both the individual devices and the broader IoT ecosystem, including networks, data storage, and third-party services.

12.   Implement strong authentication and access controls: Ensure that all IoT devices use strong authentication mechanisms, such as multi-factor authentication, and implement robust access controls to limit who can interact with the devices and their data. Replace default passwords with strong, unique passwords for each device.

13.   Secure network communications: Use encryption for all data transmitted between IoT devices and other systems. Implement virtual private networks (VPNs) or other secure communication protocols to protect data in transit. Consider segmenting IoT devices onto separate network segments to isolate them from other critical systems.

14.   Keep devices updated: Regularly update IoT device firmware and software to address known vulnerabilities. Implement a patch management process to ensure that all devices receive timely updates. For devices that cannot be easily updated, consider implementing additional security controls or replacing them with more secure alternatives.

15.   Implement device hardening: Configure IoT devices securely by disabling unnecessary features and services, closing unused ports, and implementing the principle of least privilege. Use device hardening guidelines provided by manufacturers or industry standards organizations.

16.   Monitor and analyze device behavior: Implement continuous monitoring of IoT devices to detect anomalies and potential security incidents. Use security information and event management (SIEM) tools to collect and analyze log data from IoT devices and related systems.

17.   Develop an incident response plan: Create a comprehensive incident response plan that addresses IoT-

specific scenarios. This plan should outline procedures for detecting, containing, and mitigating security incidents involving IoT devices.

18.   Implement data protection measures: Encrypt sensitive data stored on IoT devices and in associated databases. Implement data minimization principles to collect and retain only the necessary data. Ensure that data handling practices comply with relevant privacy regulations.

19.   Conduct regular security assessments: Perform periodic security assessments of your IoT ecosystem, including vulnerability scans and penetration testing. These assessments should evaluate both the technical security of the devices and the overall security of the IoT deployment.

20. Consider IoT security platforms: Evaluate and implement IoT security platforms that provide centralized management, monitoring, and security controls for IoT devices. These platforms can help streamline security operations and provide visibility into your IoT ecosystem.

21. Educate employees: Provide training to employees on IoT security best practices, including how to securely use and manage IoT devices in the workplace. Ensure that employees understand the potential risks associated with IoT and their role in maintaining security.

22. Develop an IoT security policy: Create a comprehensive IoT security policy that outlines guidelines for the procurement, deployment, use, and decommissioning of IoT devices. This policy should align with your organization's overall cybersecurity strategy and address IoT-specific concerns.

23. Implement secure boot and code signing: Where possible, use IoT devices that support secure boot mechanisms to ensure that only trusted firmware and software can run on

the device. Implement code signing to verify the authenticity and integrity of software updates.

24. Use IoT-specific security protocols: Implement IoT-specific security protocols and standards, such as the MQTT (Message Queuing Telemetry Transport) protocol with TLS encryption for secure communication between IoT devices and servers.

25. Implement API security: Many IoT devices and systems rely on APIs for communication. Implement strong API security measures, including authentication, encryption, and rate limiting, to protect against unauthorized access and attacks.

26. Consider blockchain for IoT security: Explore the potential of blockchain technology to enhance IoT security. Blockchain can provide a decentralized and tamper-resistant ledger for IoT device management, authentication, and data integrity.

27. Implement physical security measures: Protect IoT devices from physical tampering by implementing appropriate physical security controls, such as locked enclosures, tamper-evident seals, and surveillance systems.

28. Conduct supply chain risk management: Assess the security practices of IoT device manufacturers and service providers. Implement a robust supply chain risk management process to ensure that IoT devices and components meet your organization's security requirements.

29. Implement secure decommissioning procedures: Develop and follow secure procedures for decommissioning IoT devices when they reach the end of their lifecycle. This should include securely wiping data from devices and revoking their access credentials.

30. Stay informed about IoT security developments: The IoT security landscape is rapidly evolving. Stay informed about new threats, vulnerabilities, and security best practices by subscribing to relevant security publications, attending conferences, and participating in industry forums.

As IoT adoption continues to grow, organizations must also be prepared to address emerging challenges and technologies. Some areas to watch include:

5. 5G networks: The rollout of 5G networks will enable faster, more reliable connections for IoT devices, but may also introduce new security challenges related to network slicing and edge computing.

6. Artificial Intelligence (AI) and Machine Learning (ML) in IoT: The integration of AI and ML in IoT devices and systems can enhance functionality and security but may also introduce new vulnerabilities and privacy concerns.

7. Quantum computing: The development of quantum computers may pose a threat to current encryption methods used in IoT security, necessitating the adoption of quantum-resistant cryptography.

8. IoT botnets: As the number of IoT devices grows, so does the potential for large-scale IoT botnets that can be used for distributed denial-of-service (DDoS) attacks and other malicious activities.

9. Regulatory landscape: Evolving regulations related to IoT security and data privacy may require organizations to adapt their IoT security practices to ensure compliance.

Managers play a crucial role in ensuring the security of their organization's IoT deployments. To effectively manage IoT security risks, managers should:

14. Advocate for IoT security: Promote the importance of IoT security within the organization and ensure that it is given appropriate attention and resources.

15. Foster collaboration: Encourage collaboration between IT, security, operations, and other relevant departments to address IoT security holistically.

16. Prioritize security in IoT procurement: Ensure that security requirements are a key consideration when selecting and procuring IoT devices and services.

17. Support ongoing education: Encourage and support ongoing education and training for staff involved in IoT deployment and management.

18. Regularly review IoT security posture: Conduct periodic reviews of the organization's IoT security posture and ensure that security measures are keeping pace with evolving threats and technologies.

19. Align IoT security with business objectives: Ensure that IoT security initiatives align with and support the organization's overall business objectives and risk tolerance.

By implementing these best practices and staying vigilant to emerging threats and technologies, organizations can harness the benefits of IoT while effectively managing the associated security risks. As IoT continues to transform business operations, a proactive and comprehensive approach to IoT security will be essential for protecting sensitive data, maintaining operational integrity, and preserving customer trust in an increasingly connected world.

CHAPTER TWENTY-ONE: Social Engineering Awareness

Social engineering is a critical aspect of cybersecurity that often goes overlooked in favor of technical solutions. However, it remains one of the most potent weapons in a cybercriminal's arsenal. This chapter delves into the world of social engineering, exploring its various forms, techniques, and the devastating impact it can have on businesses. More importantly, it provides managers with the knowledge and tools to build a robust defense against these human-centric attacks.

At its core, social engineering is the art of manipulating people into divulging confidential information or performing actions that compromise security. Unlike technical hacking methods that exploit system vulnerabilities, social engineering targets the human element – often considered the weakest link in any security chain. Cybercriminals who employ social engineering tactics understand human psychology and exploit natural tendencies such as trust, fear, and the desire to be helpful.

The threat of social engineering cannot be overstated. According to numerous cybersecurity reports, a significant portion of successful cyberattacks involve some form of social engineering. These attacks can lead to data breaches, financial losses, reputational damage, and in some cases, complete business shutdown. What makes social engineering particularly dangerous is its ability to bypass even the most sophisticated technical security measures. After all, the most secure firewall in the world is useless if an employee willingly hands over their login credentials to an attacker.

Social engineering attacks come in various forms, each designed to exploit different human vulnerabilities. Understanding these different types is crucial for developing effective countermeasures. Some of the most common forms of social engineering include:

Phishing: This is perhaps the most well-known form of social engineering. Phishing attacks typically involve sending emails that appear to be from legitimate sources, such as banks, social media platforms, or even colleagues. These emails often create a sense of urgency and prompt the recipient to click on a malicious link or download an infected attachment. Spear phishing is a more targeted form of this attack, where the attacker customizes the message using personal information about the victim to make it more convincing.

Pretexting: In this type of attack, the cybercriminal creates a fabricated scenario to obtain information from the target. For instance, an attacker might pose as an IT support technician and call an employee, claiming there's an urgent security issue that requires immediate attention. The attacker then uses this pretext to request sensitive information or access to systems.

Baiting: This technique involves offering something enticing to the target in exchange for information or access. A classic example is leaving infected USB drives in public places, hoping curious individuals will plug them into their computers. In a business context, an attacker might offer a free software download that contains malware.

Quid Pro Quo: Similar to baiting, this attack involves offering a service or benefit in exchange for information. For example, an attacker might pose as an IT support person and offer to help with a common technical problem in exchange for login credentials.

Tailgating: Also known as piggybacking, this physical social engineering tactic involves an unauthorized person following an authorized individual into a restricted area. In an office setting, this could be as simple as an attacker holding a box and asking an employee to hold the door open for them.

Watering Hole: This sophisticated attack involves compromising a website frequently visited by the target organization's employees. When employees visit the infected site, their systems become compromised, allowing the attacker to gain access to the organization's network.

Social engineering attacks often follow a common pattern, regardless of the specific technique used. Understanding this pattern can help in identifying and preventing such attacks. The typical steps in a social engineering attack are:

1. Information Gathering: The attacker researches the target organization and its employees, often using publicly available information from social media, company websites, and other sources.

2. Relationship Building: The attacker may attempt to establish a relationship with the target, either online or in person, to build trust.

3. Exploitation: Once trust is established, the attacker exploits this relationship to manipulate the target into divulging information or performing actions that compromise security.

4. Execution: The attacker uses the obtained information or access to carry out their ultimate goal, whether it's stealing data, installing malware, or gaining further access to systems.

To combat social engineering attacks effectively, organizations need to adopt a multi-faceted approach that combines technology, policy, and most importantly, human awareness. Here are some key strategies that managers can implement to protect their organizations:

Employee Education and Training: The first and most crucial line of defense against social engineering is a well-informed workforce. Regular training sessions should be conducted to educate employees about various social engineering tactics, how to identify them, and what to do when they suspect an attack. This training should not be a one-time event but an ongoing process that evolves with the changing threat landscape.

Training sessions should cover topics such as:

- Identifying phishing emails and websites

- Proper handling of sensitive information

- The dangers of oversharing on social media

- Physical security practices, such as challenging unfamiliar faces in restricted areas

- The importance of verifying identities before providing information or access

To make training more effective, consider using real-world examples and simulations. Conduct mock phishing exercises to test employee awareness and provide immediate feedback and additional training to those who fall for the simulated attacks.

Create a Security-Aware Culture: Beyond formal training, managers should strive to foster a culture of security awareness within their organizations. This involves regularly communicating about security issues, celebrating employees who successfully identify and report potential threats, and ensuring that security is seen as everyone's responsibility, not just the IT department's.

Encourage open communication about security concerns and create a non-punitive environment where employees feel comfortable reporting suspicious activities or their own mistakes. Remember, an employee who reports clicking on a suspicious link is far more valuable than one who stays silent out of fear of repercussions.

Implement Strong Policies and Procedures: Develop and enforce clear policies regarding the handling of sensitive information, access controls, and response procedures for suspected social engineering attacks. These policies should cover areas such as:

31. Password management and multi-factor authentication

32.   Email and internet usage guidelines

33.   Procedures for verifying identities before providing information or access

34.   Guidelines for sharing information on social media

35.   Incident reporting procedures

Ensure that these policies are regularly reviewed and updated to address new threats and changes in the organization's technology landscape.

Leverage Technology: While technology alone cannot prevent social engineering attacks, it can play a crucial role in detecting and mitigating them. Implement robust email filtering systems to catch phishing attempts, use anti-malware software to detect malicious attachments, and employ network monitoring tools to identify unusual activities that might indicate a compromise.

Consider implementing Data Loss Prevention (DLP) solutions to monitor and control the flow of sensitive information within and outside the organization. These tools can help prevent employees from inadvertently sharing confidential data with unauthorized parties.

Control Information Access: Implement the principle of least privilege, ensuring that employees only have access to the information and systems necessary for their roles. Regularly review and update access permissions, especially when employees change roles or leave the organization.

Be Mindful of Public Information: Regularly audit the information your organization makes publicly available. While transparency is important, be cautious about sharing details that could be used by attackers to craft convincing social engineering schemes. This includes information about organizational structure, employee roles, and technical details about your IT infrastructure.

Physical Security Measures: Don't forget about physical social engineering tactics. Implement and enforce physical security measures such as visitor logs, employee badges, and access-controlled areas. Train reception staff and security personnel to properly verify visitors' identities and purposes.

Incident Response Plan: Develop a comprehensive incident response plan that includes procedures for dealing with suspected social engineering attacks. This plan should outline steps for reporting incidents, containing potential breaches, and communicating with affected parties. Regularly test and update this plan to ensure its effectiveness.

Vendor Management: Extend your social engineering awareness efforts to your vendors and partners. Ensure that they have adequate security measures in place and that their employees are trained to recognize and resist social engineering attempts. Remember, a breach at a vendor could potentially compromise your organization's data.

Stay Informed: The tactics used by social engineers are constantly evolving. Stay informed about new social engineering techniques and emerging threats. Subscribe to cybersecurity newsletters, participate in industry forums, and consider joining information-sharing organizations specific to your industry.

Lead by Example: As a manager, it's crucial that you model good security behavior. Follow security protocols, participate in training sessions, and openly discuss the importance of security awareness. Your attitude towards security will set the tone for your entire team.

While these strategies can significantly reduce the risk of social engineering attacks, it's important to remember that no defense is perfect. Cybercriminals are constantly developing new tactics, and even the most security-aware employee can have a momentary lapse in judgment. Therefore, it's crucial to have a layered defense strategy that can detect and respond to attacks that do manage to bypass preventive measures.

One effective approach is to create a human firewall within your organization. This involves designating and training specific employees to act as security champions. These individuals receive advanced security training and serve as points of contact for their colleagues when they encounter suspicious activities. They can help verify the legitimacy of requests, provide guidance on security best practices, and act as a bridge between employees and the IT security team.

Another important aspect of defending against social engineering is understanding the psychological tactics that attackers use. By recognizing these tactics, employees can be better equipped to resist manipulation attempts. Some common psychological tactics employed by social engineers include:

Authority: Attackers often pose as figures of authority, such as executives or IT administrators, to pressure employees into complying with their requests.

Scarcity: Creating a sense of urgency or limited availability can pressure individuals into making hasty decisions without proper verification.

Social Proof: Attackers may claim that others in the organization have already complied with their request, leveraging the human tendency to follow the crowd.

Liking: By building rapport and appearing likable, attackers can lower their targets' guard and increase the likelihood of compliance.

Reciprocity: Offering a small favor or gift can create a sense of obligation in the target, making them more likely to comply with subsequent requests.

Fear: Threats of negative consequences, such as account suspension or legal action, can panic individuals into hasty actions.

By educating employees about these tactics, you can help them recognize when they're being manipulated and encourage them to pause and verify before taking action.

It's also crucial to address the potential for insider threats, whether intentional or unintentional. While most employees have no malicious intent, they may inadvertently become insider threats if they fall victim to social engineering attacks. On the other hand, disgruntled employees or those with financial motivations might intentionally compromise security. To mitigate these risks:

10.   Implement robust access controls and monitoring systems to detect unusual activities.

11.   Conduct regular security clearance reviews for employees with access to sensitive information.

12.   Develop clear offboarding procedures to ensure that departing employees' access is promptly revoked.

13.   Foster a positive work environment to reduce the likelihood of employees becoming malicious insiders.

As organizations increasingly adopt remote work policies, the risk of social engineering attacks may increase. Remote workers may be more vulnerable to attacks as they operate outside the protected corporate network and may have less immediate access to IT support. To address this:

20.   Provide additional training for remote workers on securing their home networks and recognizing social engineering attempts.

21.   Implement strong VPN policies and multi-factor authentication for accessing corporate resources.

22.   Establish clear communication channels for remote workers to verify requests or report suspicious activities.

23. Regularly remind remote workers about the importance of maintaining a professional mindset, even when working from home.

Finally, it's important to recognize that social engineering awareness is not just about preventing attacks – it's also about building resilience. Even with the best defenses, some attacks may succeed. The goal is to create an environment where employees can quickly recognize when they've been compromised and feel empowered to report it immediately. This rapid response can significantly mitigate the damage of a successful attack.

Social engineering remains one of the most significant threats to organizational security. By understanding the tactics used by attackers, implementing comprehensive awareness programs, and fostering a culture of security consciousness, managers can significantly reduce their organization's vulnerability to these human-centric attacks. Remember, in the fight against social engineering, your employees are not just potential vulnerabilities – they are your most valuable assets in detecting and preventing attacks.

Human-centric security is an ongoing process that requires continuous effort, adaptation, and vigilance. By prioritizing social engineering awareness and making it an integral part of your organization's security strategy, you can create a more resilient and secure environment capable of withstanding the ever-evolving threats in the digital landscape.

CHAPTER TWENTY-TWO: Cybersecurity Insurance

In today's digital landscape, where cyber threats are becoming increasingly sophisticated and prevalent, organizations are recognizing the need for an additional layer of protection beyond traditional cybersecurity measures. This is where cybersecurity insurance, also known as cyber liability insurance or cyber risk insurance, comes into play. This chapter explores the concept of cybersecurity insurance, its importance for businesses, and what managers need to know when considering and implementing such policies.

Cybersecurity insurance is a specialized form of coverage designed to protect businesses from the financial fallout of cyber incidents. These policies typically cover a range of costs associated with data breaches, network damage, and other cyber-related incidents. As the frequency and severity of cyberattacks continue to rise, cybersecurity insurance has become an essential component of many organizations' risk management strategies.

The primary purpose of cybersecurity insurance is to transfer some of the financial risks associated with cyber incidents from the insured organization to the insurance provider. While it does not replace the need for robust cybersecurity measures, it can provide a financial safety net in the event of a successful attack or breach.

Cybersecurity insurance policies can vary widely in terms of coverage, exclusions, and costs. Generally, these policies may cover:

1. Data Breach Costs: This includes expenses related to notifying affected individuals, providing credit monitoring services, and managing public relations in the aftermath of a data breach.

2. Business Interruption: Coverage for lost income and extra expenses incurred if a cyberattack disrupts normal business operations.

3. Cyber Extortion: Costs associated with responding to ransomware attacks or other forms of cyber extortion.

4. Data Recovery: Expenses related to restoring or recreating data lost due to a cyber incident.

5. Legal Fees and Regulatory Fines: Coverage for legal expenses and regulatory penalties resulting from a cyber incident.

6. Forensic Investigation: Costs associated with investigating the cause and extent of a cyber incident.

7. Liability Claims: Protection against third-party claims resulting from a data breach or other cyber incidents.

When considering cybersecurity insurance, managers should be aware of several key factors:

Risk Assessment: Before purchasing a policy, it's crucial to conduct a thorough risk assessment of your organization's cybersecurity posture. This will help you understand your potential vulnerabilities and the types of coverage you may need. Insurance providers will often require this assessment as part of the underwriting process.

Coverage Limits and Exclusions: Carefully review the policy's coverage limits and exclusions. Some policies may have sub-limits for specific types of incidents or exclude certain types of attacks. For example, some policies may not cover incidents caused by unpatched software vulnerabilities or employee negligence.

Retroactive Coverage: Consider whether the policy provides retroactive coverage. This is important because cyber incidents may not be discovered immediately. Retroactive coverage can protect you from incidents that occurred before the policy was purchased but were discovered after.

Incident Response Planning: Many insurers require policyholders to have an incident response plan in place. This plan should outline the steps your organization will take in the event of a cyber incident. Some insurance providers offer assistance in developing these plans or provide access to incident response resources.

Claims Process: Understand the claims process before you need to use it. Know what steps you need to take immediately following an incident to ensure your claim will be valid. This may include notifying the insurer within a specific timeframe or using approved vendors for incident response.

Premiums and Deductibles: Like any insurance policy, cybersecurity insurance comes with premiums and deductibles. The cost can vary widely based on factors such as your industry, size, revenue, and risk profile. Be prepared to balance the cost of the policy against the potential financial impact of a cyber incident.

Policy Renewal: The cybersecurity landscape is constantly evolving, and so are insurance policies. Be prepared for potential changes in coverage and premiums at renewal time, especially if your organization has experienced a cyber incident or if there have been significant changes in the threat landscape.

Continuous Improvement: Insurance providers often require policyholders to maintain certain security standards. This can serve as an incentive for continuous improvement of your cybersecurity posture. Be prepared to demonstrate ongoing efforts to enhance your security measures.

When implementing cybersecurity insurance, managers should consider the following steps:

- Engage Stakeholders: Involve key stakeholders from across the organization, including IT, legal, finance, and risk management teams. Each of these departments will have valuable insights into the potential risks and coverage needs.

- Conduct a Thorough Risk Assessment: Work with your IT and security teams to conduct a comprehensive risk assessment. This should identify your critical assets, potential vulnerabilities, and the potential impact of various types of cyber incidents.

- Review Existing Policies: Before purchasing a standalone cybersecurity insurance policy, review your existing insurance coverage. Some general liability or property insurance policies may offer limited cyber coverage. Understanding your current coverage can help you identify gaps that need to be addressed.

- Research Providers: Not all insurance providers are equal when it comes to cybersecurity coverage. Look for providers with experience in your industry and a track record of handling cyber claims. Consider working with an insurance broker who specializes in cybersecurity insurance.

- Customize Your Coverage: Work with your insurance provider to tailor the policy to your organization's specific needs. This may involve negotiating coverage limits, deductibles, and specific policy terms.

- Develop Incident Response Procedures: Create or update your incident response plan to align with the requirements of your insurance policy. Ensure that all relevant staff members are familiar with these procedures.

- Implement Required Security Measures: If your policy requires specific security measures, such as multi-factor authentication or regular security audits, ensure these are implemented across your organization.

- Train Employees: Educate your staff about the insurance policy, including what types of incidents are covered and the steps they should take if they suspect a cyber incident.

- Regular Policy Review: Schedule regular reviews of your cybersecurity insurance policy to ensure it remains adequate as your organization and the threat landscape evolve.

While cybersecurity insurance can provide valuable protection, it's important to remember that it is not a substitute for robust cybersecurity practices. Insurance should be viewed as part of a comprehensive risk management strategy that includes strong technical controls, employee training, and incident response planning.

Managers should also be aware of some potential drawbacks and limitations of cybersecurity insurance:

Coverage Gaps: No insurance policy covers every possible scenario. There may be gaps in coverage that leave your organization exposed to certain types of risks.

Compliance Requirements: Some policies may have strict compliance requirements. Failing to meet these requirements could result in denied claims.

Increasing Premiums: As cyber incidents become more frequent and costly, insurance premiums are likely to increase. This could make coverage more expensive over time.

Exclusions for State-Sponsored Attacks: Many policies exclude coverage for incidents attributed to state-sponsored actors. Given the increasing prevalence of such attacks, this could leave organizations vulnerable.

Difficulty in Attributing Attacks: In the aftermath of a cyber incident, it can be challenging to definitively attribute the attack to a specific actor. This can complicate the claims process, especially if certain types of attacks are excluded from coverage.

Potential for Moral Hazard: There's a concern that the presence of insurance could lead to complacency in cybersecurity practices. It's crucial to maintain strong security measures regardless of insurance coverage.

The cybersecurity insurance market is still relatively young and evolving rapidly. As such, managers should stay informed about emerging trends and developments in this space. Some areas to watch include:

Parametric Insurance: This type of insurance provides a pre-determined payout based on specific triggering events, rather than requiring a lengthy claims adjustment process. This could lead to faster payouts in the event of a cyber incident.

Quantitative Risk Modeling: Insurers are developing more sophisticated models to quantify cyber risk. This could lead to more accurate pricing and tailored coverage options.

Increased Regulatory Scrutiny: As cybersecurity insurance becomes more prevalent, regulators are likely to pay more attention to this market. This could lead to new standards and requirements for both insurers and policyholders.

Integration with Cybersecurity Services: Some insurance providers are beginning to offer integrated cybersecurity services along with their policies. This could include threat intelligence, incident response support, and security assessments.

Silent Cyber Coverage: There's an ongoing effort in the insurance industry to address "silent cyber" risks - cybersecurity exposures that are neither explicitly included nor excluded in traditional insurance policies. This could lead to changes in how cyber risks are covered across various types of insurance policies.

As cyber threats continue to evolve and increase in frequency and severity, cybersecurity insurance is likely to become an increasingly important tool for businesses of all sizes. However, it's crucial to approach this type of insurance with a clear understanding of its benefits, limitations, and requirements.

Managers play a critical role in determining whether cybersecurity insurance is right for their organization and, if so, in implementing it effectively. This involves not only understanding the technical aspects of cybersecurity but also being able to assess and communicate about risk at an organizational level.

Effective implementation of cybersecurity insurance requires a cross-functional approach, bringing together expertise from IT, security, legal, finance, and risk management. Managers need to facilitate this collaboration, ensuring that all relevant perspectives are considered in the decision-making process.

Moreover, managers need to view cybersecurity insurance as part of a broader risk management strategy. This involves balancing investment in preventative measures with insurance coverage, and continuously reassessing this balance as the threat landscape evolves.

Cybersecurity insurance can provide valuable protection against the financial impacts of cyber incidents. However, it's not a silver bullet. It works best when combined with strong cybersecurity practices, a culture of security awareness, and a proactive approach to risk management. By understanding the role of cybersecurity insurance and implementing it thoughtfully, managers can help their organizations become more resilient in the face of ever-evolving cyber threats.

CHAPTER TWENTY-THREE: Monitoring and Auditing Your Security Posture

In the ever-evolving landscape of cybersecurity, implementing robust security measures is only half the battle. The other crucial component is continuously monitoring and auditing your security posture to ensure that your defenses remain effective against emerging threats. This chapter delves into the importance of ongoing security monitoring and auditing, providing managers with essential insights into maintaining a strong security stance.

Security monitoring and auditing are proactive approaches to cybersecurity that involve continuously assessing and evaluating your organization's security controls, processes, and overall posture. These practices help identify vulnerabilities, detect potential security incidents, and ensure compliance with internal policies and external regulations.

The primary goal of security monitoring is to maintain real-time awareness of your organization's security status. This involves collecting and analyzing data from various sources across your network to detect and respond to potential security threats promptly. On the other hand, security auditing is a more formal and periodic process that involves a comprehensive review of your security measures to ensure they meet established standards and remain effective.

Implementing a robust security monitoring program requires a multi-faceted approach. Here are key components that managers should consider:

Security Information and Event Management (SIEM): A SIEM system is a cornerstone of effective security monitoring. It collects and analyzes log data from various sources across your network, including firewalls, intrusion detection systems, servers, and applications. SIEM tools use advanced analytics to identify patterns and anomalies that may indicate a security threat.

When implementing a SIEM solution, it's crucial to properly configure it to collect relevant data and generate meaningful alerts. This often requires fine-tuning over time to reduce false positives and ensure that critical events are not overlooked. Additionally, ensure that your team is trained to effectively use the SIEM tool and interpret its outputs.

Network Traffic Analysis: Monitoring network traffic is essential for detecting unusual patterns or potential threats. Network traffic analysis tools can help identify signs of malware communication, data exfiltration attempts, or other suspicious activities.

Consider implementing tools that provide deep packet inspection capabilities, allowing you to examine the content of network traffic for potential threats. However, be mindful of privacy considerations and ensure that your network monitoring practices comply with relevant regulations.

Endpoint Detection and Response (EDR): With the increasing prevalence of remote work and bring-your-own-device (BYOD) policies, endpoint security has become more critical than ever. EDR tools monitor endpoint devices for signs of compromise and can provide valuable insights into potential security incidents.

When selecting an EDR solution, look for features such as real-time threat detection, automated response capabilities, and integration with your existing security infrastructure. Ensure that your EDR solution covers all types of endpoints used in your organization, including mobile devices and IoT devices where applicable.

User and Entity Behavior Analytics (UEBA): UEBA tools use machine learning algorithms to establish baseline behaviors for users and entities within your network. They can then detect anomalies that may indicate a compromised account or insider threat.

When implementing UEBA, it's important to establish accurate baselines for normal behavior. This may require a period of "learning" during which the system observes typical patterns of activity. Be prepared to refine and adjust the system over time to reduce false positives while ensuring that genuine anomalies are detected.

Vulnerability Scanning: Regular vulnerability scans help identify potential weaknesses in your systems and applications before they can be exploited by attackers. Automated vulnerability scanning tools can provide a continuous view of your security posture and help prioritize patching efforts.

Implement a regular schedule for vulnerability scans, ensuring that all critical systems and applications are covered. Consider both internal and external scans to get a comprehensive view of your vulnerabilities. Establish a process for prioritizing and addressing identified vulnerabilities based on their severity and potential impact on your organization.

Threat Intelligence Integration: Incorporating threat intelligence into your monitoring efforts can provide valuable context and help you stay ahead of emerging threats. Threat intelligence feeds can provide information on new vulnerabilities, attack techniques, and indicators of compromise.

When selecting threat intelligence sources, consider a mix of open-source feeds and commercial services relevant to your industry. Ensure that your security team has the capability to effectively consume and act on threat intelligence, integrating it into your existing monitoring and response processes.

While continuous monitoring provides real-time insights into your security posture, periodic security audits offer a more comprehensive and structured evaluation of your security measures. Here are key aspects of security auditing that managers should be aware of:

Types of Security Audits: There are several types of security audits, each serving a specific purpose:

1. Compliance Audits: These ensure that your organization meets the requirements of relevant regulations and industry standards, such as GDPR, HIPAA, or PCI DSS.

2. Technical Audits: These involve a detailed examination of your technical controls, including firewalls, access controls, encryption implementations, and network configurations.

3. Process Audits: These evaluate the effectiveness of your security processes and procedures, such as incident response plans, change management processes, and user access reviews.

4. Physical Security Audits: These assess the security of your physical premises, including access controls, surveillance systems, and environmental controls.

When planning your audit schedule, consider conducting a mix of these audit types to ensure comprehensive coverage of your security posture.

Audit Planning and Scope: Effective audits require careful planning and a clear definition of scope. Determine which systems, processes, and locations will be included in the audit. Establish the objectives of the audit and the criteria against which your security measures will be evaluated.

Consider involving stakeholders from various departments in the planning process to ensure that all relevant areas are covered. Clearly communicate the audit scope and objectives to all affected parties to set expectations and facilitate cooperation.

Audit Execution: During the audit, auditors will gather evidence through various means, including document reviews, interviews with staff, system configuration checks, and vulnerability assessments. It's important to provide auditors with the necessary access and resources to conduct a thorough evaluation.

Encourage your staff to be open and cooperative during the audit process. Remember that the goal is to improve your security posture, not to assign blame. Foster a culture where audits are seen as opportunities for improvement rather than punitive measures.

Audit Reporting and Follow-up: The audit report should provide a clear picture of your current security posture, highlighting both strengths and areas for improvement. It should include detailed findings and recommendations for addressing any identified issues.

Upon receiving the audit report, develop a plan to address the identified issues, prioritizing based on risk and potential impact. Assign responsibilities and timelines for implementing the recommended improvements. Establish a process for tracking the progress of these improvements and verifying their effectiveness.

Continuous Improvement: Use the insights gained from both continuous monitoring and periodic audits to drive ongoing improvements in your security posture. This may involve updating policies and procedures, implementing new security controls, or providing additional training to staff.

Foster a culture of continuous improvement within your security team. Encourage regular reviews of security measures and processes, and be open to new ideas and technologies that can enhance your security posture.

Managers play a crucial role in ensuring the effectiveness of security monitoring and auditing efforts. Here are some key responsibilities:

Resource Allocation: Ensure that your security team has the necessary resources to implement and maintain effective monitoring and auditing programs. This includes allocating budget for tools and technologies, as well as investing in training and development for your security staff.

Risk Assessment and Prioritization: Work with your security team to assess the risks facing your organization and prioritize monitoring and auditing efforts accordingly. Focus on protecting your most critical assets and addressing the most significant threats first.

Fostering a Security-Conscious Culture: Promote a culture of security awareness throughout your organization. Encourage all employees to be vigilant and report potential security issues. Ensure that security considerations are integrated into all aspects of your business operations.

Compliance Oversight: Stay informed about the regulatory requirements applicable to your organization and ensure that your monitoring and auditing efforts align with these requirements. Work closely with your legal and compliance teams to address any regulatory concerns.

Incident Response Preparedness: Ensure that your organization has a well-defined incident response plan in place. Regularly review and update this plan based on insights gained from monitoring and auditing activities. Conduct periodic drills to test the effectiveness of your incident response procedures.

Vendor Management: If you rely on third-party vendors for security monitoring or auditing services, ensure that they meet your organization's security requirements. Regularly review their performance and security practices to minimize the risk of vendor-related security incidents.

Reporting to Stakeholders: Regularly communicate the results of monitoring and auditing activities to relevant stakeholders, including senior management and the board of directors. Provide clear, concise reports that highlight key risks and the steps being taken to address them.

Staying Informed: Keep yourself updated on emerging security threats and best practices. Attend industry conferences, participate in professional networks, and encourage your security team to engage in continuous learning and development.

As the threat landscape continues to evolve, so too must your approach to security monitoring and auditing. Here are some emerging trends and considerations to keep in mind:

Artificial Intelligence and Machine Learning: AI and ML technologies are increasingly being integrated into security monitoring tools, enabling more sophisticated threat detection and anomaly identification. Consider how these technologies can enhance your monitoring capabilities, but also be aware of their limitations and potential biases.

Cloud Security Monitoring: As more organizations move their infrastructure and applications to the cloud, cloud security monitoring becomes crucial. Ensure that your monitoring efforts extend to your cloud environments and that you have visibility into cloud-specific security events.

IoT Security: The proliferation of Internet of Things (IoT) devices introduces new security challenges. Ensure that your monitoring and auditing efforts encompass IoT devices and the unique risks they present.

Privacy Considerations: With increasing privacy regulations, it's important to balance security monitoring needs with privacy requirements. Ensure that your monitoring practices comply with relevant privacy laws and respect individual privacy rights.

Security Orchestration, Automation, and Response (SOAR): SOAR platforms can help streamline and automate security operations, including incident response. Consider how SOAR technologies can enhance your monitoring and response capabilities.

Human-Centric Security: While technology plays a crucial role in security monitoring, the human element remains critical. Invest in developing the skills and expertise of your security team, and foster a security-aware culture throughout your organization.

Effective security monitoring and auditing are essential components of a robust cybersecurity strategy. By implementing comprehensive monitoring systems and conducting regular audits, organizations can maintain a strong security posture, detect and respond to threats promptly, and continuously improve their defenses.

Managers play a vital role in this process, ensuring that the necessary resources are allocated, fostering a security-conscious culture, and staying informed about emerging threats and best practices. By prioritizing security monitoring and auditing, organizations can build resilience against cyber threats and protect their valuable assets in an increasingly complex digital landscape.

Remember that security is an ongoing journey, not a destination. Continuous monitoring, regular audits, and a commitment to improvement are key to maintaining a strong security posture in the face of evolving cyber threats. By embracing these practices and fostering a culture of security awareness, organizations can enhance their ability to detect, respond to, and mitigate security risks effectively.

CHAPTER TWENTY-FOUR: Staying Ahead of Emerging Threats

In the rapidly evolving landscape of cybersecurity, staying ahead of emerging threats is a constant challenge for businesses of all sizes. As technology advances, so do the tactics and tools employed by cybercriminals. This chapter explores the importance of proactive threat intelligence, emerging threat vectors, and strategies for maintaining a robust security posture in the face of evolving risks.

The cybersecurity landscape is characterized by its dynamic nature. Threats that were once considered cutting-edge quickly become commonplace, while new, sophisticated attack methods continually emerge. This constant evolution necessitates a proactive approach to threat identification and mitigation.

One of the key elements in staying ahead of emerging threats is the effective use of threat intelligence. Threat intelligence involves collecting, analyzing, and disseminating information about current and potential cybersecurity threats. This information can come from a variety of sources, including:

1. Open-source intelligence (OSINT): Publicly available information from news sources, social media, and online forums.

2. Commercial threat intelligence feeds: Paid services that provide curated and analyzed threat data.

3. Government and industry-specific information sharing centers: Organizations that facilitate the exchange of threat information within specific sectors.

4. Internal security data: Information gathered from an organization's own security systems and incident response activities.

The goal of threat intelligence is to provide actionable insights that allow organizations to make informed decisions about their security strategies. This can involve identifying new types of malware, understanding the tactics and motivations of threat actors, or recognizing emerging attack patterns.

To effectively leverage threat intelligence, organizations need to establish a structured process for collecting, analyzing, and acting on this information. This process typically involves the following steps:

- Collection: Gathering raw data from various sources.

- Processing: Organizing and standardizing the collected data.

- Analysis: Examining the processed data to identify patterns, trends, and potential threats.

- Dissemination: Sharing relevant insights with appropriate stakeholders within the organization.

- Action: Implementing necessary changes to security policies, controls, or practices based on the intelligence gathered.

It's important to note that not all threat intelligence is equally relevant or actionable for every organization. The key is to focus on intelligence that is most pertinent to your specific industry, geographic location, and technology stack.

One of the emerging trends in threat intelligence is the use of artificial intelligence (AI) and machine learning (ML) to enhance the collection and analysis of threat data. These technologies can help organizations process vast amounts of data more quickly and accurately, identifying subtle patterns and connections that might be missed by human analysts.

However, it's crucial to remember that AI and ML are tools to augment human intelligence, not replace it entirely. Human expertise remains essential in interpreting the context and implications of threat intelligence and making strategic decisions based on that information.

As organizations work to stay ahead of emerging threats, it's important to be aware of some of the key areas where new risks are likely to emerge. These include:

36.   Internet of Things (IoT) vulnerabilities: As more devices become connected to the internet, the potential attack surface for cybercriminals expands. Many IoT devices lack robust security features, making them attractive targets for attackers looking to gain a foothold in corporate networks.

37.   5G network risks: The rollout of 5G networks promises increased speed and connectivity, but it also introduces new security challenges. The distributed nature of 5G architecture and the increased reliance on software-defined networking create new potential vulnerabilities.

38.   Artificial Intelligence-powered attacks: Just as AI can be used to enhance cybersecurity defenses, it can also be leveraged by attackers to create more sophisticated and targeted attacks. AI-powered malware that can adapt to evade detection is a growing concern.

39.   Quantum computing threats: While still in its early stages, quantum computing has the potential to break many of the encryption algorithms currently used to secure data. Organizations need to start considering quantum-resistant cryptography to protect against future threats.

40.   Supply chain attacks: As organizations strengthen their own security measures, attackers are increasingly targeting vulnerabilities in the supply chain. This can

involve compromising third-party software or hardware to gain access to multiple organizations simultaneously.

41.   Deepfake technology: Advanced AI-generated audio and video content (deepfakes) could be used to enhance social engineering attacks, making it more difficult for employees to distinguish between legitimate and fraudulent communications.

42.   Cloud security challenges: As more organizations move their infrastructure and data to the cloud, securing these environments becomes increasingly complex. Misconfigurations and inadequate access controls in cloud environments can lead to significant data breaches.

To effectively address these and other emerging threats, organizations need to adopt a proactive and adaptive approach to cybersecurity. This involves several key strategies:

14.   Continuous monitoring and assessment: Regularly evaluate your organization's security posture, including vulnerability assessments and penetration testing. This helps identify weaknesses before they can be exploited by attackers.

15.   Rapid patching and updates: Establish processes for quickly implementing security patches and updates across all systems and devices. Many successful attacks exploit known vulnerabilities for which patches are already available.

16.   Security awareness training: Regularly educate employees about emerging threats and best practices for cybersecurity. Human error remains a significant factor in many successful cyberattacks, making ongoing training essential.

17.   Incident response planning: Develop and regularly test incident response plans that address a wide range of potential scenarios, including emerging threat vectors. This

helps ensure that your organization can respond quickly and effectively to new types of attacks.

18.   Collaboration and information sharing: Participate in industry-specific information sharing groups and collaborate with peers to stay informed about emerging threats and best practices for mitigation.

19.   Investing in advanced security technologies: Consider implementing advanced security solutions such as Next-Generation Firewalls (NGFW), Endpoint Detection and Response (EDR) systems, and Security Information and Event Management (SIEM) platforms. These tools can provide enhanced visibility and protection against sophisticated threats.

20.   Adopting a zero-trust security model: Move away from the traditional perimeter-based security approach and implement a zero-trust model that verifies every user, device, and application attempting to access resources, regardless of their location.

21.   Embracing security automation: Implement security orchestration, automation, and response (SOAR) tools to streamline security operations and enable faster response to potential threats.

22.   Focusing on data protection: Implement strong data protection measures, including encryption, access controls, and data loss prevention (DLP) solutions. As data becomes increasingly valuable, protecting it from theft and unauthorized access is crucial.

23. Cultivating a security-minded culture: Foster a culture of security awareness throughout the organization, encouraging all employees to take an active role in protecting company assets and data.

One of the challenges in staying ahead of emerging threats is the need to balance proactive security measures with business operations and innovation. Overly restrictive security policies can hinder productivity and slow down the adoption of new technologies that could provide competitive advantages.

To address this challenge, organizations should adopt a risk-based approach to security. This involves:

24. Identifying and prioritizing critical assets and data.

25. Assessing the potential impact of various types of threats on these assets.

26. Implementing security controls that are proportionate to the level of risk.

27. Regularly reviewing and adjusting security measures based on changes in the threat landscape and business needs.

This approach allows organizations to focus their resources on protecting their most valuable assets while maintaining the flexibility to adopt new technologies and business practices.

Another important aspect of staying ahead of emerging threats is the development of a robust threat hunting program. Threat hunting involves proactively searching for signs of malicious activity within an organization's networks and systems, rather than waiting for automated alerts or incident reports.

Effective threat hunting requires a combination of skilled personnel, advanced analytics tools, and a deep understanding of both the organization's environment and the tactics used by potential attackers. By actively seeking out hidden threats, organizations can detect and respond to sophisticated attacks that might otherwise go unnoticed.

As organizations work to stay ahead of emerging threats, it's also important to consider the role of regulatory compliance. Many industries are subject to specific cybersecurity regulations, and these regulations are continually evolving to address new threats and technologies.

Staying compliant with these regulations is not only a legal requirement but can also provide a framework for implementing robust security practices. However, it's important to remember that compliance alone does not guarantee security. Organizations should view regulatory requirements as a baseline and strive to exceed these standards where appropriate.

The rapid pace of technological change also means that organizations need to be prepared for the security implications of emerging technologies. For example:

9. Edge computing: As more processing moves to the edge of networks to support IoT devices and reduce latency, new security challenges arise in protecting these distributed computing resources.

10. Blockchain: While blockchain technology offers potential security benefits, it also introduces new risks and challenges, particularly in areas such as key management and smart contract vulnerabilities.

11. Extended Reality (XR): As virtual and augmented reality technologies become more prevalent in business environments, they introduce new privacy and security concerns that organizations need to address.

12. Autonomous systems: The increasing use of autonomous systems in various industries raises questions about security, liability, and ethical decision-making that organizations need to consider.

Staying ahead of these and other emerging technologies requires ongoing education and collaboration between security teams, IT departments, and business leaders. Organizations should establish processes for evaluating the security implications of new technologies before adopting them, and for continuously monitoring and adjusting security measures as these technologies evolve.

In conclusion, staying ahead of emerging threats is a complex and ongoing challenge that requires a multifaceted approach. By leveraging threat intelligence, adopting proactive security strategies, and fostering a culture of security awareness, organizations can enhance their ability to detect, prevent, and respond to new and evolving cyber threats. However, it's important to remember that no security measure is foolproof, and the landscape of cyber threats will continue to evolve. The key to long-term success lies in building a flexible and resilient security posture that can adapt to new challenges as they emerge.

CHAPTER TWENTY-FIVE: Building a Cybersecurity Culture

In the complex world of cybersecurity, technology and processes are essential components of a robust defense strategy. However, one often overlooked yet crucial element is the human factor. Building a cybersecurity culture within an organization is paramount to ensuring that all employees understand their role in protecting the company's digital assets. This chapter explores the importance of fostering a security-conscious environment and provides practical strategies for managers to cultivate a cybersecurity culture that permeates every level of the organization.

A cybersecurity culture refers to a shared set of values, attitudes, and behaviors that prioritize security in all aspects of an organization's operations. It goes beyond simply implementing security policies and procedures; it's about creating an environment where security becomes second nature to every employee, from the C-suite to the newest hire.

The importance of building a cybersecurity culture cannot be overstated. Even the most advanced security technologies and well-crafted policies are ineffective if employees don't understand or adhere to them. Human error remains one of the leading causes of data breaches and security incidents. By fostering a culture of security awareness, organizations can significantly reduce their risk exposure and create a more resilient defense against cyber threats.

To build a strong cybersecurity culture, organizations need to focus on several key areas:

Leadership Commitment: The foundation of any cultural change within an organization starts at the top. Senior leadership must demonstrate a clear commitment to cybersecurity and lead by example. This involves not only allocating necessary resources but also actively participating in security initiatives and consistently communicating the importance of cybersecurity to all stakeholders.

Leaders should make cybersecurity a regular topic in company-wide meetings, include it in strategic planning discussions, and ensure that security considerations are integrated into all business decisions. By doing so, they send a clear message that cybersecurity is a top priority and an integral part of the organization's values.

Education and Training: A comprehensive and ongoing education program is essential for building a cybersecurity culture. This goes beyond annual compliance training sessions; it requires a multifaceted approach that engages employees and keeps security top of mind throughout the year.

Consider implementing the following educational initiatives:

Regular security awareness training sessions that cover a wide range of topics, from phishing and social engineering to password hygiene and data protection.

Simulated phishing exercises to test and reinforce employees' ability to recognize and report suspicious emails.

Gamification of security training to make it more engaging and memorable. This could include security-themed quizzes, challenges, or even escape room-style activities.

Lunch and learn sessions where security experts can share insights and best practices in an informal setting.

A mentorship program where security-savvy employees can guide and support their colleagues in adopting secure practices.

Clear Communication: Effective communication is crucial for building and maintaining a cybersecurity culture. Organizations should establish clear channels for disseminating security information and updates. This includes:

A dedicated intranet page or newsletter that provides regular security tips, news about emerging threats, and updates on the organization's security initiatives.

Visual aids such as posters, digital signage, or screensavers that reinforce key security messages throughout the workplace.

A system for quickly alerting employees about urgent security threats or incidents.

Open forums or town halls where employees can ask questions and share concerns about security issues.

Empowerment and Responsibility: Employees should feel empowered to take an active role in the organization's security efforts. This involves:

Encouraging employees to report suspicious activities or potential security incidents without fear of reprisal.

Recognizing and rewarding employees who demonstrate good security practices or contribute to improving the organization's security posture.

Assigning security champions within each department to serve as liaisons between the security team and their colleagues.

Involving employees in the development and review of security policies and procedures to ensure they are practical and effective.

Integration into Business Processes: Cybersecurity should not be viewed as a separate function but as an integral part of all business processes. This means:

Incorporating security considerations into the design and implementation of new projects and initiatives from the outset.

Including security metrics in performance evaluations and job descriptions across all departments.

Ensuring that security requirements are clearly communicated and enforced in vendor and partner relationships.

Regularly reviewing and updating business processes to address evolving security needs.

Continuous Improvement: Building a cybersecurity culture is an ongoing process that requires constant evaluation and refinement. Organizations should:

Regularly assess the effectiveness of their security awareness programs and adjust them based on feedback and results.

Stay informed about emerging threats and best practices, and update their security culture initiatives accordingly.

Encourage innovation in security practices by soliciting ideas from employees across the organization.

Conduct periodic surveys or focus groups to gauge employees' understanding of and attitudes towards cybersecurity.

As managers work to build a cybersecurity culture, they may encounter several challenges:

Resistance to Change: Some employees may view security measures as burdensome or unnecessary. To overcome this, managers should focus on explaining the "why" behind security policies and demonstrating how they align with the organization's overall goals.

Information Overload: With the constant flow of security alerts and updates, employees may become overwhelmed or desensitized. Managers should strive to provide concise, relevant, and actionable security information to prevent fatigue.

Balancing Security and Productivity: There's often a perceived tension between security measures and productivity. Managers need to find ways to implement security practices that enhance rather than hinder workflow efficiency.

Measuring Success: It can be challenging to quantify the effectiveness of cultural change initiatives. Managers should develop meaningful metrics that go beyond compliance numbers to measure actual behavioral changes and risk reduction.

To address these challenges and foster a robust cybersecurity culture, managers can employ several strategies:

Lead by Example: Managers should consistently demonstrate good security practices in their own work and interactions. This includes using strong passwords, being cautious with email attachments, and following proper data handling procedures.

Personalize the Message: Help employees understand how cybersecurity relates to their specific roles and responsibilities. Use real-world examples and scenarios that are relevant to their day-to-day work.

Create a Positive Security Narrative: Instead of focusing solely on the negative consequences of security breaches, highlight the positive impact of good security practices. Celebrate successes and share stories of how security measures have protected the organization.

Foster Cross-Functional Collaboration: Encourage collaboration between the security team and other departments. This can help break down silos and ensure that security considerations are integrated into all aspects of the business.

Provide Ongoing Support: Ensure that employees have access to the resources and support they need to maintain good security practices. This could include a dedicated help desk for security-related questions or a knowledge base of security best practices.

Adapt to Different Learning Styles: Recognize that employees have different learning preferences. Offer a variety of training formats, including in-person sessions, online modules, videos, and hands-on exercises, to cater to diverse learning styles.

Leverage Peer Influence: Identify and cultivate security champions within different teams or departments. These individuals can serve as role models and help reinforce security messages among their peers.

Make it Personal: Help employees understand how good cybersecurity practices can benefit them personally, both at work and in their personal lives. This can increase buy-in and motivation to adopt secure behaviors.

Use Storytelling: Share real-world stories of security incidents and their impact, both within your organization and in other companies. This can make the consequences of poor security practices more tangible and relatable.

Regularly Review and Update Policies: Ensure that security policies and procedures remain relevant and practical. Involve employees in the review process to gain their insights and increase buy-in.

Address the Human Element: Recognize that even the most security-conscious employees can make mistakes. Foster an environment where people feel comfortable admitting errors and reporting potential security issues without fear of punishment.

Integrate Security into the Employee Lifecycle: Incorporate security awareness into the onboarding process for new employees and continue to reinforce it throughout their tenure with the organization. Include security responsibilities in job descriptions and performance evaluations.

As organizations work to build a cybersecurity culture, it's important to recognize that this is not a one-time effort but an ongoing journey. The threat landscape is constantly evolving, and so too must an organization's approach to security. A truly effective cybersecurity culture is one that can adapt to new challenges and technologies while maintaining a strong foundation of security awareness and best practices.

Managers play a crucial role in this ongoing process. They must stay informed about emerging threats and trends in cybersecurity, continually assess the effectiveness of their organization's security culture initiatives, and be willing to adjust their approach as needed. This might involve embracing new technologies, updating training programs, or revising security policies to address new risks.

Moreover, as organizations increasingly adopt remote and hybrid work models, the concept of a cybersecurity culture must extend beyond the physical boundaries of the office. Managers need to ensure that the security-conscious mindset is maintained regardless of where employees are working. This may require additional training on securing home networks, using VPNs, and maintaining data privacy in shared workspaces.

Another important consideration is the role of cybersecurity culture in the context of digital transformation. As organizations adopt new technologies such as cloud computing, Internet of Things (IoT) devices, and artificial intelligence, the security landscape becomes increasingly complex. A strong cybersecurity culture can help employees navigate these changes more effectively, ensuring that security remains a priority even as the organization evolves.

Building a cybersecurity culture also involves striking a balance between security and innovation. While it's crucial to protect against threats, an overly restrictive security environment can stifle creativity and hinder business growth. Managers must work to create a culture that values both security and innovation, encouraging employees to think creatively about how to achieve business goals while maintaining robust security practices.

Ultimately, a strong cybersecurity culture is about more than just protecting against threats; it's about building trust. In an era where data breaches and cyber attacks can severely damage an organization's reputation, a demonstrated commitment to cybersecurity can be a significant differentiator. By fostering a culture where every employee understands and values the importance of security, organizations can build trust with their customers, partners, and stakeholders.

Building a cybersecurity culture is a complex but essential task for modern organizations. It requires commitment from leadership, ongoing education and communication, and the active participation of every employee. By focusing on these key areas and addressing the challenges that arise, managers can create an environment where security is not just a set of rules to follow, but a fundamental part of how the organization operates. In doing so, they not only enhance their organization's security posture but also contribute to its overall success and resilience in an increasingly digital world.

www.ingramcontent.com/pod-product-compliance
Lightning Source LLC
La Vergne TN
LVHW022342060326
832902LV00022B/4189